"When Parents Are

A Young Person'

Real Self-Protection

By

Jamie Clubb

Published by Jamie Clubb trading as Clubb Chimera Martial Arts

Editing for first edition by Ian Lewis and Robert Agar-Hutton.

Editing for second edition by Thomas Wilson with additional edits by Mary Stevens.

Cover design by Gianni Susassi based on a concept by Mim Clubb.

Clubb Chimera Martial Arts logos designed and created by Gianni Susassi and Miriam Clubb.

Photography by Mary Stevens, Christopher Webb, Chris Mort and Jamie Clubb with archive photography by Miriam Clubb

First published as an eBook by Ex-L-Ence Publishing in 2017

Second edition published as an eBook by Jamie Clubb trading as Clubb Chimera Martial Arts in 2020

Third edition published as an eBook and paperback (with additions and amendments to the text plus the inclusion of photographs for the first time) by Jamie Clubb trading as Clubb Chimera Martial Arts in 2023

Contents

Dedication

This book is dedicated to my wonderful daughter, Thalia, who once told me "Our tears are a memory that we were once part of the sea." Here's to protection against the spider-dolls of life

Message to the Parent, Guardian or Carer

This book is written with the young person in mind and it is intended to tell the truth, as it is today, regarding self-protection. Sadly, the world of self-protection teaching often gives the wrong idea by trying to provide abstract "quick fix" solutions. I view self-protection as an all-encompassing attitude to life, a set of robust principles naturally cultivated from common sense and instinct. We are all the product of countless generations of humans who made the right choices to survive. Self-protection is about being switched onto life and understanding other people. This understanding has a dual effect. Firstly, it teaches children how to perceive and handle a threat. Secondly, it improves their communication skills and self-confidence.

Self-protection is about independence developed through an honest understanding of life. Whether we like it or not most children, at some point, will be left in situations when they will have to think for themselves. Such circumstances can occur at a much earlier time in their lives than we might wish. Being on their own is a natural part of growing up, but it also means that at different periods they will be exposed to danger. A child's ability to handle that danger needs to be instinctive, but this can only be learnt through honest experience. In order to provide the most honest experience possible we need to make their training in self-protection as realistic as possible. However, such realism has to be managed in a responsible yet efficient way. This means it needs to be both safe and enjoyable at the same time in order for the information to be quickly absorbed and relevant skills learned. After all, independence is all about making decisions and it would seem like a logical start to have a child choose to learn self-protection. A good teacher can make lessons enjoyable, but it is the realism that requires the support and understanding of parents.*

I learnt fairly early on when I started training young students that a parent, guardian or carer's cooperation and encouragement is crucial. A self-protection lesson is not a crèche or "just another activity". It is as important as any other safety lesson - such as cycling proficiency, first aid or road safety - and should be viewed as such by the parent, the child and the teacher. However, in order for a parent and child to take this degree of seriousness to such an activity they need to be confident they are getting what they have signed up for. The teacher or coach has an obligation to the parent to deliver a service that is clearly designed for the purpose described.

Unfortunately this is not often the case. An industry has built up around children in the martial arts, teaching minors anything but realistic modern self-protection techniques. Important lessons, like attitude and awareness, are often glossed over and training for children mainly takes the form of learning combative techniques. However, even these techniques are often naïve at best and abstract at worst, better suited for flashy fight choreography scenes or sports. Many martial arts and even self-protection teachers will shy away from teaching actual practical self-defence physical skills to their pupils for fear of recrimination in some form.

We have seen the emergence of games in lessons that have no relevance to martial arts or self-protection whatsoever and are often included as bribes to keep a child's interest. This completely ruins the objective of the training in the first place. Imagine taking your child for football or netball practice only to find out half the lesson was taken up by another unrelated sport and that playing an actual game was rare. Unfortunately, this is the popular face of many children's martial arts classes across the western world.

You would be better off, in most cases, putting your child in a rough and tumble (but safely and responsibly managed) sport like rugby, judo, boxing, Brazilian jiu jitsu and reputable Thai boxing or mixed martial arts (MMA) schools than many classes that name "self-defence" as just one of their listed attributes. These suggestions may be sports and not self-defence, but at least they help develop fortitude through honest physical contact and a child gets a straightforward confirmation of their physical ability in an environment that will test them. Fortunately, since the first time I wrote this book I have seen the emergence of more schools across the martial arts subculture in different countries integrating more realistic and responsible children's self-protection programmes. There aren't nearly enough but progress is being made.

Self-protection should begin with honesty between all its stakeholders. Children and parents should be able to leave a lesson with justified confidence over the self-protection teacher's practical approach to a very serious subject. This confidence can only be backed up by honest feedback. A teacher needs to be able to be frank with the parent, guardian or carer at all time's about their child's ability to process and apply the material being taught.

This book may be written for children to read, but it is best read with an adult. Remember, reading and watching educational films are fine but are of little use if the information is not absorbed and put into practice. I encourage children to teach as early as possible. This gives them agency and a commitment to the material they have been taught, as well as deepening their understanding of the principles and practices. Such an approach is also intended to promote an independent mind. If self-protection is to be taken seriously it should become a part of the learner's life, a simple habit demonstrated by a confident and switched-on personality that is neither paranoid nor unaware.

*Please note: When I refer to parents I am, of course, also referring to guardians and carers.

What is Self-Protection?

When people think of the term "self-protection" or "self-defence" they often imagine scenes of fighting. The truth is that good self-protection has little to do with fighting but everything to do with surviving and thriving. A person who is good at self-protection understands how and why to avoid bad situations that will endanger themselves and their friends, whether it is at home, at school, in the outside world or online. A person who is good at self-protection will know that fighting is always the last resort but if they need to fight they will do so only to escape a dangerous situation. Above all, a person who is good at self-protection is a confident person who takes charge of his or her own actions. The following sets out terms and ideas that I will use throughout this book.

Self-Defence is legal term used to describe the use of force to prevent harm from another person. Most countries give their citizens the right to self-defence. When I use the term self-protection I am describing everything you can do to reduce the threat of someone physically harming you and what to do if you are forced to become physical. Some people call the very large non-physical part of self-

WHEN PARENTS AREN'T AROUND:
A YOUNG PERSON'S GUIDE TO SELF-PROTECTION

protection **Personal Security**. The self-defence part is the *very small* physical part of self-protection. In theory, if you get all the personal security part right then you will never have to use self-defence. However, life isn't always that simple.

The approach to self-protection taught in this book is centred on five tenets: **Respect, Awareness, Courage, Discipline** and an **Open Mind**. Each chapter in this book will add to our understanding of these and give some examples but for now here are some brief descriptions.

Respect: If we are going to defend ourselves, we need to feel like we are worth defending. I can tell you straight away that you have priceless value as a human being. There is no one else in the world like you and there is a lot of good you, as a unique individual, can do that will make a difference to the lives of many people. You deserve respect and you should respect others. However, if you do not show self-respect then some people, even people you have known to be kind, might not be respectful to you. So, when you walk, keep your head up and observe the world around you. Know in your mind exactly where you are heading. When you talk, speak clearly and with confidence. When you listen, do so with care.

Awareness: You should adopt a habit of being aware of your surroundings and aware of yourself. Always look around you and be sure of what is going on at that present time. When you talk to others be mindful of who they are, what you really know about them and what information you are telling them – be it face-to-face or online. Listen to your "gut feelings". Don't do unnecessary things that will hinder any of your senses, for example using any form of listening device when you are out in public or walking alone. Later on I will discuss the different stages of awareness. Having knowledge of these will mean that you will be best prepared if a situation changes.

WHAT IS SELF-PROTECTION?

Courage: Being brave is far more than just "having the guts" to fight. Being brave can often mean *not* fighting, especially if others are trying to force you into fighting. Courage does not mean you are fearless. In fact, when we say courage in self-protection, it means doing the right thing when you are most frightened. In self-protection, the right thing means stopping someone from harming you or another.

Discipline: Discipline is all about self-control and learning. In order to be good at anything worthwhile you need to practise hard and regularly. You need to concentrate on what is important and be prepared to push yourself, in all ways, past the point where you are comfortable. No-one became good at anything worthwhile by staying comfortable when they practised and/or trained. It is only by having good self-discipline can you really grow and be in charge of your life. Self-protection is all about being in charge when faced with dangerous or potentially dangerous situations.

Open Mind: Situations change. You must be prepared to change as well. It is a rule of nature that those who adapt survive the best. An open mind helps you understand and accept change. Self-protection situations can be life changing so if we are prepared for change then you are more likely to do the best thing when the unexpected happens. Being open-minded also means you take in more information easily and question it in a sensible way.

All these tenets are about keeping a good attitude. We want to improve your character so that you are respectful but not arrogant, aware but not nervous, courageous but not foolish, disciplined but will know when to relax, and open-minded without being gullible. I hope that this book will help you become all of these things.

Good self-protection is first about making yourself safe from violence. You do what you can to avoid violence and, if this is not immediately possible, you do what is possible to stop the violence against you quickly. It is about looking after you and taking control of a potentially bad situation. After that, it is about helping others and making them safe. We should encourage more people to be less aggressive to one another and to be more protective over their community. When people feel more part of the same community, they are less likely to want to hurt one another. That is ultimate self-protection.

Fighting

Real fights are rarely fair and they rarely solve matters, especially if you have been encouraged to take part. They are unlikely to bring an end to a bullying situation and can prolong the torment by becoming content for cyber-bullying.

Normally self-protection books deal with fighting last. They do this because you should only really fight when you have no other choices. However, to cover the lessons that I have outlined in these chapters, I feel it is important that we understand a few things about the nature of fighting. We need to understand fighting so we can best avoid it.

First of all, let me repeat what I said in the previous chapter - you only fight when it is impossible to talk or escape. This does not mean meeting someone after school or in the local park for a fight because you feel you have no other choice. Fighting people just to show how "hard" you are, or because they have challenged you, should be seen as no more than a trap.

This type of fighting a "match fight" and it has no place in effective self-protection strategies. The place for this type of fighting should only be sought within combat sports, where it is supervised and governed by clear rules. These sports can complement your self-protection training but should never be confused with actual self-defence. Self-defence is not a competition or a contest. "Match fighting" outside of combat sports is not good self-defence and you will see why in the next paragraph.

Bullies have always challenged weaker people to fight them. You will notice that it is they who make the challenge and they who pick the place and time. By doing this, they take control before the fight has even begun. They will call you a coward or a "chicken" if you do not go and their friends will back them up. You will notice that the friends don't do the fighting! Even when you enter a fight with someone you think you might have a chance of defeating, the bully has already won because he has been able to persuade you to do something they want and you don't. Remember self-protection is all about control. By accepting a fight, you have just given control to the person who has made the challenge.

The fight is not likely to be fair. In fact, it is quite probable you will end up walking straight into a set-up where your challenger will take you by surprise, use a weapon or attack you with his or her friends. Even if this doesn't happen, the bully is often stronger than you. After all that is why they have picked you to fight and that is one of the reasons why they are a bully!

Don't be fooled by the idea that, even if you lose, you will have shown you weren't a coward and will have earned some respect. This idea, if ever it was really true, came before the widespread use of social media. At the time this is being written – and I don't see it changing very soon - most unofficial match fights are recorded on various devices to be uploaded online. They will be made viral within seconds of the last strike being thrown or even streamed live as the fight is happening. The person who lost the fight or clearly received the most damage will now be targeted by online campaigns, allowing the bullying to continue after the fight.

FIGHTING

Even if you "win" an arranged unofficial match fight you can face other problems that most will not have considered when emotions were running high and the fight was agreed. For a start, you might end up with a bad permanent school record that could affect your future education. More seriously, you could end up in trouble with the law via the Juvenile Justice System for common assault, disturbing the peace, and/or various other possible offences. In the United Kingdom, children under 10 cannot be tried as criminals but can be given a Local Child Curfew – forbidding them from being in a public place between the hours of 9pm and 6am unless accompanied by an adult – or, if they break this curfew or their offence is judged by the court to be more serious be issued with a Child Safety Order where they are placed under the supervision of a Youth Offending Team. They might also be taken away from their parents or guardians to be placed into care. In England, Wales, and Northern Ireland you are considered criminally responsible from the age of 10 (it is 12 years old in Scotland) and can be arrested and taken to a youth court or they might be given a youth caution by a police officer. Although children under 18, and especially those under 16, will be treated very differently to adults who committed the same crime, a child found guilty will receive a criminal record. Cautions and criminal records can affect your ability to get a job or even work experience.

Remember, agreeing to fight someone is not the same thing as defending yourself or another person. Understanding this point is crucial to self-protection training. If you ever have to fight someone it needs to be for a reason far bigger than what others will think of you or the belief that it will stop a bully from challenging you. You will be fighting because you cannot immediately escape or you are protecting someone from harm. That is genuine self-defence and, in this case, the law is on your side.

Dealing with someone challenging you to a fight can be tough. A bully will try to make you feel like a coward for refusing to agree and it might mean that the bully will continue to challenge you, sometimes becoming more physical because they think you are afraid. The main way to deal with this is to know that you are not a coward. There is nothing brave about allowing someone to force you into doing something they want you to do simply because you are worried about what others might think about you.

The bully is the real coward for picking on you in the first place. All bullies pick fights with people they think they can beat. It takes real courage to stand up to a bully and not allow them to take control of you. Standing up to them does not mean fighting them, especially when this is what they are trying to achieve. There are several short plans that can be used to deal with such situations.

First of all, if you are a good talker, try talking them out of challenging you. Try taking them away from their friends to talk about their problem with you. By separating them from their supporters (their friends), you immediately take control and are more likely to be able to stop them from wanting to

Real fights have no rules, can result in serious injury and/or have legal consequences.

fight you. Try changing the subject. Try asking them questions. Try anything that gets them off the subject of challenging you to fight. If this distraction plan doesn't work, try pointing out how silly it is for them to fight you. Don't be afraid to point out that they are bigger than you or a better fighter. They will not be expecting this type of honesty. What they want is for you to feel so hurt by their comments that you feel you have to fight them. When you start removing things that seem obvious to them as good reasons to fight, it will be harder for them to challenge.

Try listening to the person who is making the challenge or trying to start the fight and show them you are listening. This approach only works on certain people. Some bullies aren't full-time bullies. They are just bullies in certain situations. For example, something might have happened that has upset them and made them feel weak. By picking a fight they feel strong again, although this will not last. The longer you get them to talk the more opportunities you will have for them to decide against fighting you.

I understand that all of this can seem very difficult, as you will definitely be feeling very emotional at the time. This is natural. If nothing else, take control of your breathing and make more time.

You might wish to use some noise. This plan should not be over-used, as the story of the "Little Boy who Cried Wolf" demonstrates. Only ever shout and make a noise if you really mean it and if you really feel like you are being threatened. If you do this all the time, then it is less likely that anyone will take you seriously. So, when you do make a noise or shout, make sure you do so with all seriousness. We will talk about using anger as a weapon in the chapter on the "fence". For the moment think of it as a plan to gain the attention of others and to make the bully feel uncomfortable about what he is trying to make you do. By shouting "No!" you are taking control of the situation. Bullies hate the word "No". It is a powerful word if you are prepared to stick to using it every time a bully tries to make you do something you don't want to do.

WHEN PARENTS AREN'T AROUND:
A YOUNG PERSON'S GUIDE TO SELF-PROTECTION

In Britain there is a dying custom where adults would ask each other to "step outside" to settle an argument. What they were doing was challenging each other to a fight. Upon agreeing to fight they would take off their jackets and maybe roll up their sleeves before they both fought. No one else would join in the fight and often there would be rules. This came from the British tradition of boxing when it was taught to gentlemen, and some ladies, in the 18th and 19th centuries. However, today very few people actually fight this way unless they are at a boxing club or in a boxing match. The rules of real fights have changed. In the real world THERE ARE NO RULES! Do not be fooled into thinking you are "saving face" by fighting in an unarmed duel - which is what these types of boxing contest were in the past. The chances are you will be taking your first of many beatings.

A bully relies on you choosing to fight them. Don't be scared to say things like "Why should I fight you? You'll probably beat me up." Few bullies expect this response. They are hoping to shame you into fighting them. There is no shame in telling everyone what the bully is really thinking or telling everyone the reality of the situation: here is a stronger person trying to make a weaker person fight him or her. The story of "The Emperor's New Clothes" shows us the virtue of speaking the truth when everyone else is too scared.

Human beings are the most intelligent animals on the planet. However, sometimes we act just like other mammals. The "match fight" is an example of this mammalian behaviour. Some self-protection experts call this the "monkey dance". Monkeys and other primates often have fights to decide the boss of the group. Sometimes this is just done through intimidation and a fight doesn't actually happen. Often, however, they wrestle and the bigger monkey wins to become chief of the group. Monkeys and other animals do this because they live in a harsh and primitive world where they mainly rely on their instincts. They do not know any better and do not want anything more from life. Most of the time we have the choice not to act like monkeys and we should always do our best to exercise that choice. So, when you see someone trying to pick a fight or challenging someone to fight, think of them as monkeys doing their dance.

As I said before, fighting should be kept inside the boxing or wrestling gym or the martial arts club. There is nothing wrong with doing this in a fair and organised competition, if you choose to do so, and there are trustworthy adults there to control everything. However, these matches should never be done to make another person feel bad or to make you feel better than them. They should be done as a way to test our abilities and to enjoy a sport. In my lessons we regularly "spar" so we can test certain things. We box, we kick-box, we grapple, and we do various self-defence pressure tests, but this is always done in a friendly environment, where there is no bullying and we all understand we are doing this to improve our skills and not to hurt our training partners. I believe if more people did this type of training they would not want to fight in real life. You can prove yourself in training and do not need to hurt others to feel good.

Respect: You need to respect yourself enough to not let someone else control a situation where you will end up getting hurt.

Awareness: A very different type of awareness here. You should be aware of what is happening when someone is challenging you to fight or trying to arrange one with you. They are behaving like an animal that wants to prove themselves to the group by hurting someone smaller than them. Also be aware of those involved who will not be fighting (such as the fight challenger's "friends"). They just want entertainment at your expense.

Courage: Because "match fighting" once had a place in our culture, where people "defended their honour" or "righted a wrong" by fighting another person, we often worry about others thinking us cowardly for not accepting a fight. Real courage comes from being able to fight those emotions and standing up to a bully by not agreeing to meet them for a fight or play their game.

Discipline: Real discipline in a challenge situation means that you will stick fast to your decision not to meet and fight the bully - and only fight them if you have no other choice, for example, if they try to attack you there and then. In this case, you will use your discipline to remember that you are fighting to get away from the bully. Discipline in fight training comes from doing it again and again so that you really push yourself in your abilities. It also means learning and training to do your best to avoid fighting in the first place.

Open Mind: Having an open mind will help you think about why someone decides they want to fight and why fighting someone on their terms is not such a great idea. They say that every good general chooses his or her battlefield. Choose yours wisely. In other words make your battlefield the world of thinking - make the bully think - and it will be less easy for a bully to want to fight.

Life's Warning Signs

Our bodies were developed in prehistory for a time that was very different from today. Humans evolved from a time when they hunted wild animals with primitive tools for food and resources and were also hunted *by* other wild animals. Humans and their ancestors also had to face other tribes in battles of life-and-death. This was happening before humans had even evolved into humans. We are still biologically best suited for this existence where every day was a fight for survival.

Since our bodies have not moved on much from this time, we experience emotions that we call "fear" and "worry". Because these words used for emotions came out of times when we didn't understand the science, such feelings were viewed as being bad. We also get unusual sensations when we sense something is wrong.

WHEN PARENTS AREN'T AROUND:
A YOUNG PERSON'S GUIDE TO SELF-PROTECTION

These sensations are sometimes called "gut feelings", as they often make our stomachs feel strange. Because we often can't make sense of them, we frequently ignore them or, worse still, get annoyed with ourselves for feeling them. However, when we lived in more savage times, we understood that these strange feelings were signals to help us. They are part of what we call "instinct".

From one point of view it is a good thing that most of us are not as used to these feelings. It means that we live in a much safer world. Unfortunately, it also means that we can endanger ourselves by not paying attention to these natural warning signals. Sometimes people are so unfamiliar with these feelings of fear that they put themselves at risk by ignoring them or their lack of understanding makes them become worried about everything. We do not want either of these behaviours. We need to understand what these signals warn us about and what we should do when we feel them.

Imagine you are walking down a street and a teenage boy, who has been standing with a couple of other people of similar age, approaches you and asks for the time. You suddenly get a bad feeling in your stomach and it makes you tingle all over. This person hasn't been rude to you and is asking you a very normal thing. However, you really don't feel comfortable answering him, instead you feel that you want to move away and suddenly you find yourself running away. This sounds like a pretty ridiculous reaction to someone just asking you for the time but on this occasion your instincts were protecting you.

Afterwards, when discussing the matter with your parents, you realise that the teenager who spoke to you had a menacing smirk on his face, he seemed to be moving towards you a little too fast (almost like he was about to chase you), and he had been standing with two other boys - surely wouldn't at least one of them have had the time? You also remember that you had just been messaging someone on your new phone when you first noticed his approach. He could have been after your device or just after trouble full stop. You recall hearing about similar incidents happening in the area. What has happened is that your mind has quickly seen the potential threat and hit you with a signal to escape rather than explaining to you the things that make sense now. This is what is meant when people say, "Your instincts take over".

What we are talking about is a natural signal evolved for us to survive in an ancient world where there was very little time to make decisions. When a situation really gets serious - such as when you know someone wants to hurt you - there is no time to think about making a decision. Thinking too much about something in these moments can cost you dearly. Once your instinct talks to you it means that your body is getting ready to do something pretty dramatic. It might want to run, it might want to fight, or it might want to freeze.

Of these three, running or simply getting away from a situation is nearly always the body's favourite reaction because this means you are getting away from any potential harm. When we cannot run - just like most animals - we fight. A lot of people will fight when they are involved in a violent situation but what happens is that they start fighting when it is too late and their chances of escaping are slim. There are a lot of arguments over why we freeze. Some say it is so that we can hide better. This would have been particularly good in prehistoric times when a large wild animal might have chased us and our stillness helped us to camouflage. Others say it is so that we could play dead if a big animal got hold of us; they would think we were no longer alive and the animal would stop attacking and give us enough time to make a sneaky escape. Whatever the reason, freezing is rarely a good option when faced with the potential threat of another human being.

Recently experts on trauma have added fawn and flop to this list. Fawn is a response where we try to please and befriend the person trying to hurt us, whilst flop is when we lose total control of our bodies – even blacking out. Fawning has proven to be effective for some people who are being held against their will, such as in a kidnapping situation. Flopping might be the body's extreme version of "playing dead".

Flight   Fight   Freeze   Fawn   Flop

When we lived in more primitive times, we understood our gut feelings very well. Like animals, we used them to our advantage. We felt the threat and responded with the right action. Today we still get these feelings, not only when something is life threatening but also from less serious things too. However, there is no point in being scared of everything because that is not healthy. You have to understand what is actually causing you to feel fear.

For example, you might be scared of spiders. This could come from any number of reasons. Spiders are predators in real life. They are pretty scary to other creatures around their size and smaller, which they might prey upon. Of the 650 species of spider resident in the UK only 12 of these can cause harm to humans. However, bites are extremely rare. When they do occur it usually causes nothing more than some short-lived irritation or swelling around the bitten area. Only in extreme and rare cases can the most venomous of these species, the female noble false widow, cause enough pain and discomfort for you to be sent to hospital. Infection from bites is usually the biggest concern and, as with any wound, a person who has been bitten should clean the affected area. Usually false widow bites are no worse than receiving a wasp or bee sting and are currently far less likely to happen than either of those two.

In fact, most spiders worldwide do not pose a threat to humans. However, if you saw an unusual looking spider in Australia you might have a good reason to be wary - some very deadly spiders live in that country and their bite can be fatal. This is what we call "in context". Your fear of spiders in Australia is perfectly rational and is "in context"; though most Australians live amongst these deadly animals in a calm state of awareness. Your fear of spiders in general is irrational and "out of context" and it might be signs of a phobia that can be overcome with the right training.

Your instincts may warn you about something at any time. All you need to decide is whether or not you are being warned about a real danger or not. Think of it like an alarm people have in their houses and cars. Most of the time when it goes off nothing is wrong. The alarm has just detected movement; it could be a cat walking past the sensor, for example. However, the alarm was designed to alert its owners of intruders or car thieves and sometimes that is exactly what it does. Your "gut feelings" or instincts are your body's natural alarm system. This book should help guide you through typical and general rules of self-protection, which should help you understand when to obey your instincts.

Respect: Respecting your body's warning signs by taking notice of them is what I would call Inner-Respect. Outer-Respect is not letting others push you into doing something you don't feel comfortable with, particularly if you don't trust the person. Respect your "gut feelings" (inner-respect) and respect your right to choose not to do something against your will (outer-respect).

Awareness: There are two types of awareness in self-protection: self-awareness and situational awareness. Self-awareness is practised when you begin to understand the reason why your body naturally acts as it does during times of danger. By being self-aware, you are more likely to be in control of a situation. Situational awareness is when you properly recognise the danger that your body's feelings are warning you about. For example, your gut is telling me that a certain person could be dangerous even though they haven't threatened you.

Courage: When you know something is wrong, it often takes courage to act - the act may be to run or it may be to shout. Most people actually worry more about being embarrassed than they do about getting hurt. If you believe your instincts are right then you need to do something right away. Get used to taking action even if that action is simply asking for help.

Discipline: Discipline is required to not let your instincts completely rule you. Sometimes your instincts are so busy at keeping you safe they actually hold you back. You may need to face your fears in order to improve your survival skills - such as with physical training to make you stronger - and that means good self-control.

Open Mind: If you have a closed or narrow mind, it is very easy to deny your instincts in an otherwise innocent looking situation. Take the example I described earlier with the teenagers who asked you for the time. An open mind allowed you to look beyond their normal-sounding question and helped get you to safety.

Spotting the Warning Signs in Others

The human body is incredible. We have already talked about how it can alert you to possible dangers. However, we have also said that it may warn you about things that really are not a serious threat. We also need knowledge to better understand whether another human being is a threat or not. Luckily nature has done a good job in doing this too.

Attackers will either use deception first to trick you or they will reveal their aggressive intentions prior to attacking. Sometimes they might do a combination of the two. Deception is used to get you to lower your defences so they can get to you easier and strike before you have time to react. Aggression is usually the

attacker losing control of their emotions prior to physically attacking you. However, this approach might also be used to intimidate so that you will submit easier and be too afraid to fight back.

Remember, just because someone is a possible attacker or a potential threat it does not necessarily mean they will attack you or are intending to attack you. However, it is important to recognise the warning signs early so that you have more time to handle the situation.

<u>Deceptive Warning Signs</u>

Those who deceive are often trying to take control of you. They seek to manipulate you. For example, this is quite often the way some people sell things you might not want. However, when your "gut feeling" and your common sense tells you something is wrong it can be because someone you don't trust is trying to control you. This might be someone talking you into buying something or it might be something far worse.

The word "conman" or "con-woman" normally makes us think of people who sell dodgy products. However, conmen and women can also be people who use techniques to fool you into trusting them so they can hurt you. Remember, attackers don't always want your property. The word "con" comes from the term "confidence trickster". This means someone who tricks you into having confidence in them. They "win your confidence" so that they can use you to do something they want, but you might not. Here are some warning signs of this type of person:

"We"
Watch out for a person who uses the word "we" too much. These are people who try to make out you and they are somehow in the same situation or in the same gang when this is not true. Controllers

do this so that you will lower your mental defences and be friendlier. This allows them to control you more. It is up to you whether or not you wish to be friendly with someone. Remember, most people are nice and are just doing this to get to know you as a friend, but always be aware of this first tactic.

Flattery

For hundreds and hundreds of years wise writers have warned us about flatterers. A flatterer or a charmer is someone who says nice things to you in order to get what they want. Look up the story of "The Fox and the Crow" by Aesop to see how a cunning fox tricked a crow out a piece of cheese by flattering the bird into singing by complimenting him on his "beauty". The crow had the cheese in his beak and, once he sang, out fell the cheese and the fox caught it. The story warns us

Beware when a person uses the word "we" to make you feel like you are both part of the same team.

about people who flatter us to get what they want. Watch out for compliments. They can be nice and genuine, but sometimes they are just tactics to win your trust. Always think about where these flattering comments are coming from and whether you felt comfortable before the person started flattering you.

Small Insults

If flattery doesn't work sometimes people use small insults. They might say something like "I guess you are too scared" in order to get you to do something you do not want to do. This tactic works by getting you to prove the insult to be wrong. "I guess someone *like you* is too much of a goody-goody" is a classic example that many people – both children and adults – use to get you to ignore advice about safety taught by your parents and teachers. Remember, all these small insults are being used so that the insulter can control you.

Unwanted Favours

Watch out for unwanted favours. This is when someone offers to help you with something when you haven't asked them. This can be used against you later. Sales people do this all the time when they give out free gifts in order that you feel you have to buy from them to return the favour. Perhaps someone offers to carry your bag when you haven't asked and you can clearly manage it on your own. Again, the important thing to remember here is context and how you feel when they offer their help. Offering a favour that isn't needed or required is an old control method.

Beware when someone insists on helping you with something when it is clear help is not needed.

Stories

Watch out for those who spin out a story. Liars often talk too much to convince themselves that their story sounds believable. It is like when you know someone who tries to get off going to school because they have a headache and they go into describing how it feels without being asked. You know they are lying because when you are really ill you don't really want to talk too much about it and just want to get better. Likewise the lying controller will spin out a detailed story in order to make it sound good to them. For example, a person trying to convince you to go somewhere with them might give you a long, detailed explanation of the place.

Promises

Be wary of promises you haven't asked for such as "I promise you will be alright". There are two reasons why someone might say this to you. The most obvious one is so that you won't be scared of being hurt. However, the second reason shows that they do not really believe what they are saying and by promising it makes it sound more convincing to them.

Ignoring "No"

Finally, and most importantly, watch out for people who do not take "No" for an answer. Of all the controlling methods, the surest one that gives away that someone really wants to control you is if they ignore you when you say "No". Try to think of "No" as a powerful word that forms its own sentence with no other words needed to follow: N.O. with a full stop: "No." It does not require an explanation to follow. When you say it, you have made your position clear on the matter. You never need to give excuses or reasons why. When someone ignores your strong wishes

"No" means NO and that is the end of it.

on something that concerns you, they are giving you a very big warning sign. No means **NO** and that is the end of it.

WHEN PARENTS AREN'T AROUND:
A YOUNG PERSON'S GUIDE TO SELF-PROTECTION

Aggressive Warning Signs

Violence is when someone uses physical force against another. When someone attacks you they might not always do it with violence. They might use threats or intimidation without touching you. However, some attackers will think nothing of hurting you physically. Luckily there are very often clear, natural signals that give away when someone really wants to cause you physical harm.

All Talk

When someone shows you anger, they don't always want to physically hurt you. This is the same with animals. A cat or a dog might hiss or bark to make you stay away but if they really wanted to hurt you they would probably just attack. When someone is making a noise, such as shouting and yelling at you, but not

actually getting close to you the chances are they do not really want to get physical. When we cover the idea of the "fence", I will talk more about how we can use distance as part of a self-protection tactic. When an unarmed person wants to get physical they often need to get close. They might scream at you, call you names, use swearing and insult you in the nastiest way possible but if they are staying where they are and not making moves to come forward, you know that they do not really want to get physical.

24

SPOTTING THE WARNING SIGNS IN OTHERS

Sometimes people use shouting and aggression or anger to get themselves ready to attack but what this often does is the exact opposite. The longer they shout and scream, the less likely they are to get physical.

Eyes Bulging and Other Angry Signs

Many species of animal use wide-eyed stares to scare off their enemies. When we get very angry, our eyes can sometimes seem to bulge in our heads. Often it is just a warning but many scientists have theorised that the bulge-eyed stare comes from a person under stress experiencing tunnel vision. Tunnel vision is when someone's vision narrows and the eyes try to take in as much as possible in order to focus on what is causing them to feel stress. The person might also puff their chest up, push their chin forward and splay their arms. Chest puffing and arm splaying are usually warning-off signs; the

Arm splaying is usually a warning off posture.

person is trying to appear larger. They put their chin forward as if to dare you to hit them or showing they do not fear you. All of these signs are usually just for show and only become dangerous should

A particularly dangerous sign to spot is when an aggressor's hands start clenching or they ball into fists.

25

you move towards them, forcing them to back up their threats.

Their face might also become red because the blood has rushed to this part of their body. Again, this doesn't automatically mean the aggressor or angry person wishes to become physical. In fact, some experts on human behaviour believe such a sign indicates far less danger than someone whose face has suddenly drained of colour in a moment of anger. This paler-faced act of aggression could be a sign that the blood has moved away from the head and into parts of the body that are being readied for violence. Angry people might also spit as they talk and shout as they are forgetting to swallow due to the excitement of the moment. Their whole bodies often stiffen as they brace themselves for physical impact. A particularly dangerous sign to spot is when an aggressor's hands start clenching or they ball into fists.

Understanding that an angry person does not always intend to be violent, no matter what they are saying or how they are gesturing, is important. However, what is more important is not to provoke them further. Keep out of their space and let them have their tantrum for now.

Attack Signs

When an angry attacker becomes physical they will often use their words as they cover the distance between the two of you. For example, they will say something like "What are you looking at?" as they walk into your space or they will shove you and shout something like "Come on then!" or grab you to make their demand. For example, "Give me your phone!" The secret here is to not let them cover that distance. Again, we will cover this in the "fence" chapter.

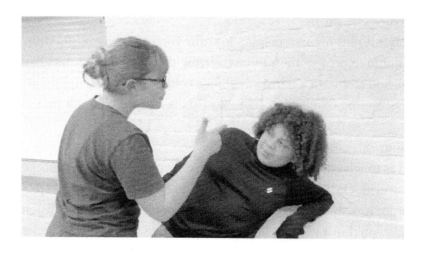

Allowing an aggressive and verbally abusive person to get too close puts you at their mercy. Should they choose to become physical, you will have fewer opportunities to do anything to stop them.

Short Words

Another sign you can spot when someone wants to get physical - and this is part of the "monkey dance" - is when they start shortening their words. This signals the conversation is really over. All the angry person wants to do is fight. They use very short words like "yeah", "and", and "C'mon then!" Swearing is also very common. They don't often make much sense but this is because their brain is only thinking about getting their body to fight. When these words come and someone is getting close: the attack is coming very, very soon. Their mouth may be speaking but they really don't want to talk with you.

Other Signs

More dangerous signs in an aggressive person usually include several behaviours that appear to be the opposite of the earlier angry display signs. This is because the aggressor is getting ready to fight and is not putting on a display to warn you off. They might drop their chin to protect their throat, furrow their brow to protect their eyes, and step into a narrower stance (rather than splaying their arms). Seeing their hands ball into fists is a more obvious sign.

Online

It is much easier for people to use deception online than in the real world. Online people can pretend to be something they are not in order to win your trust. Be aware of people trying to get you to do things you don't want to do and observe the same signals described earlier in this chapter. Report anything that gives you reason to be worried about another person's online behaviour to your parents, such as requesting your personal information. We will cover this again in the "Stalkers" section of the next chapter.

When online, it is tempting to behave quite differently from how we act in the world outside. We can easily feel we are protected and can say what we want to other people without apparent or immediate consequences. People are often rude in a way they never would be if they were talking to another person face-to-face. Many threats online, as they are in real life, are just words and people behaving angrily. However, threatening behaviour should always be reported. Although you and others might not be in immediate danger, a person making threats can still be a violent person. Immediately inform your parents. Keep records, such as screen shots, of their threats and inform the administrators of the game or social media platform you are using.

Respect: Respect how serious the situation is when someone either tries to control you or behaves in an aggressive way. It is also about respecting yourself enough not to fall for the controller's tricks or being frightened into becoming the angry attacker's prey.

Awareness: Be aware of what is happening by reading the warning signals a controller or angry attacker gives off.

Courage: Now that you have the knowledge, you can use it to stop the controller playing their game with you. You will also need to use courage to stand your ground against the angry attacker and make the best choice at that particular moment to either escape or fight.

Discipline: You will need discipline to stay in control. Your emotions may pull you this way and that when you are in a real situation. You will need to be disciplined to stick to your knowledge and not let a possible attacker become an actual attacker. A good way to develop discipline is to practise with role-play exercises at your martial arts or self-protection club, with your friends, or with your parents.

Open Mind: Keep your mind open to the idea that people use either controlling tricks or aggression to get their way. By being open to this idea you will be able to spot the methods early on and act the right way. Having an open mind will also allow you to look outside of self-protection at the way people use controlling and angry methods to get their own way. This might happen in your home and in your own friendships. You can stop others from behaving this way, and stop yourself too, in order help create a fairer environment.

Different Types of Attacker

Human beings act in all sorts of ways when they want to attack you. They also have different reasons – what we might call motives. These motives can be important because they can affect the way you choose to deal with the person. Below are just a few of examples of attackers. Although all might be regarded as a type of bully, they aren't the type of person who challenges you to a fight. They are predators who aren't really interested in proving themselves but who use violence to get something.

Muggers

Muggers are thieves that rob people by making them feel afraid of being physically hurt or by actually physically hurting them. They come in all sorts of shapes and sizes, and are of all different ages. They may be strangers, they may be people you know and they might even be a relation. Some muggers commit this crime because they are lazy bullies who have found that it is easier to get things off people who are scared of them rather than working in an honest job.

WHEN PARENTS AREN'T AROUND:
A YOUNG PERSON'S GUIDE TO SELF-PROTECTION

Some people do it because they are addicted to a substance, such as drugs, and need the money. Substance addicted muggers are often desperate people, driven to a life of crime. Some muggers are people who simply enjoy hurting people first and then taking their money or property off them as an extra benefit. All three are very serious threats, but the last one is the most dangerous from a self-protection point of view.

The reason for this is because the first two types of mugger mostly only want money from you or something they can sell, whereas the last type wants to hurt you and take your property only as a type of trophy. However, the other two can be just as dangerous if they simply decide that attacking you to get what they want is better than just scaring you.

Thugs

A thug is a type of violent bully. The word "thug" originally came from a murderous Indian cult known as the Thuggee. However, when I say "thug" I mean a person who is out to cause trouble because he or she wants to feel important, and violence is the only way that they think they can achieve this feeling. A good number of people who use violence have grown up in a violent family and/or neighbourhood where people get their own way by using force. Maybe an older brother or sister or one of their parents bullies them. Perhaps the street they live in or their local community sees a lot

of fighting. They have many different ways to attack, but in most cases it starts with intimidation - in other words they want to make sure you are scared of them.

Kidnappers

A kidnapper is usually - but not always - an adult. There are different reasons for kidnapping a child. In a few cases, a criminal wants to kidnap someone in order to get money from their parents. This is not common in most countries. In some cases, the kidnapper wants to hurt the child. In other cases, the kidnapping is performed to cause grief for a parent. In most cases, kidnappers are someone the child knows and it is usually a close relative.

There are three basic ways of kidnapping someone:

- Taking someone by surprise and running or driving off with him or her. This is the method most people imagine when it comes to kidnapping. It happens but it is quite rare compared to the other two methods.
- Scaring someone into going with them by using threats and aggression.
- Tricking someone into going with them by telling lies, using flattery or offering promises (see the previous chapter). This can be done in-person and via social media, where the kidnapper has a lot of time to build up trust in their intended victim. Overall this third method is most common as the kidnapper is usually someone the victim knows or thinks they know.

Sometimes a kidnapper will use a combination of two or even all three of these tactics. The kidnapper might try to trick their victim into thinking it is okay to go with them or they might do just enough to get close to the victim and then suddenly take them by surprise. If trickery is not working, the kidnapper might abruptly change their plans and become aggressive, and then either frighten the victim into going with them or simply take them by force. Another method might be to go from being aggressive to appearing to be nice before pouncing. There are many different methods a kidnapper might use, but it is important that we understand the three basic ways listed above, so we can identify them in a real situation if it ever happens.

Most kidnappers will use some form of deception or trickery. They are very often someone the victim knows very well.

Sometimes, kidnappers will use outright aggression.

Tell your parents that you always want to know if someone different is going to pick you up from school, your club or wherever you may be left without them. If your parents don't live together, always be clear about the times when the parent you don't usually live with is picking you up. This should be done either before they drop you off or by phoning the adults responsible for looking after you, such

as your teachers. Know your schedule and be aware of the schedule changing. Be clear about what day of the week it is, what date it is and what is planned for you on each day.

Intruders

An intruder is someone who tries to get into your home without the permission of your parents. They can also try to get into other places, such as your parents' car. Their methods may be similar to the kidnapper. They might be sneaky and slip in like a burglar. This might happen because they think no one is in the home or to take those living in the home by surprise. They might use aggression, although this is not common. They will - in most cases - be deceptive and try to fool you into letting them inside. Like the kidnapper, this deception might come in many forms. They might lie that they know your parents and your parents know they are coming over. They might say they are here to check the electricity, water or gas. These people should never go into a house where only a child is present. Think of your house as you and your parents' castle and no-one else is allowed in unless you are sure they have your parents' permission. Make sure your parents let you know who is and who is not allowed in your home when they are not there.

Pests

A pest is someone who annoys you and gives you unwanted attention. When we talk about pests in self-protection, we do not mean just anyone who annoys you, but someone who makes you uncomfortable by what they say or do. This might be someone who touches you when you do not want them to and continues to do so even when you tell them to stop. They might not touch you but just talk to you about things that make you feel uncomfortable and continue to do so

when you tell them to stop. They might use some of the deceptive methods we discussed in the last chapter. These people should always be reported to your parents and/or teachers. Remember, your body is your own.

Stalkers

A stalker is a type of pest that follows you. They might physically follow you and look into your business, including your personal life. This might take the form of cyber-stalking where they follow you online. Again, this type of behaviour should not be tolerated. Report the person

stalking you to your parents and/or teachers. When you are online be very careful about not revealing personal information in your profile, as well as in public and private discussions. Do not engage in private discussions with people you do not know. Make sure you understand the privacy settings for whatever social media platform or game you are using.

DIFFERENT TYPES OF ATTACKER

Remember, all of the above types of attacker are breaking the law so it is very important that you report the individuals.

Respect: Respect yourself by not allowing others to deceive or intimidate you, or make you feel uncomfortable. Respect others by not becoming an unwanted pest. Remember: if you want others to respect your boundaries, you need to respect theirs too.

Awareness: Be aware of what types of people are out there, so you are ready to act before they do.

Courage: There are lots of situations discussed in this chapter where you will need to be brave and not give in. Remember, you have no reason to trust someone who has not given you any good reason to trust them or their motives.

Discipline: You have already shown discipline in reading to this point. Now keep that discipline by storing the knowledge in your head and practising it regularly.

Open Mind: As with the last chapter, keep an open mind that there are muggers, thugs, kidnappers, intruders and pests in life. However, it is also worth remembering that there are far more nice people in the world than those who want to steal and hurt. Do not scare yourself by thinking that there are more people who want to hurt others than those who don't. This isn't true and thinking this way isn't helpful for your self-protection training. We will discuss the difference between awareness and hyperawareness in the next chapter.

WHEN PARENTS AREN'T AROUND:
A YOUNG PERSON'S GUIDE TO SELF-PROTECTION

A Special Chapter on Awareness

In this chapter we are going to concentrate on what it means to be aware in the real world. This means being switched on and alert. Overall, it is good to be aware of your surroundings: to know where the car is parked; how to get home; and what is going on in your local community. These are all examples of basic awareness. However, for self-protection your awareness is about spotting people who are genuine **Immediate Confirmed Threats**. The sooner you can recognise a possible threat, the faster you can avoid or manage a dangerous situation.

What is an Immediate Confirmed Threat?

An immediate confirmed threat is someone who has the capability, opportunity and intention to seriously hurt you. So, your school friend might be physically strong enough to hurt you and can easily get to you but you have no reason to believe he or she would wish you any harm. You might meet a toddler who becomes very angry with you and wants to lash out. The little child can get you and clearly wants to really hurt you but they don't have reasonable capability to do any serious harm. Finally, imagine a violent criminal who has been imprisoned on the other side of the world for attacking people who have your hair colour. They may have the capability to hurt you and may want to attack you but they cannot get to you. Therefore, an immediate threat is typically someone who is big enough to cause you damage, has the opportunity to get to you and their behaviour has led you to believe they wish to cause you physical harm.

WHEN PARENTS AREN'T AROUND:
A YOUNG PERSON'S GUIDE TO SELF-PROTECTION

The man might have the capability and opportunity to cause harm but his behaviour demonstrates no intent.

The man has the capability, opportunity and intent to cause harm. He is an immediate confirmed threat.

The man might have the intent and the opportunity to cause harm but his leg splint makes him incapable of being an immediate possible threat.

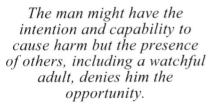

The man might have the intention and capability to cause harm but the presence of others, including a watchful adult, denies him the opportunity.

As I mentioned in the first chapter, there are different stages of awareness. An American firearms pistol coach called Jeff Cooper divided these up into four colours to explain which stage and what action we can and should take in any situation.

Code White

Code white is the state of being unaware. This is when you are switched off. Some examples might be when you are at home relaxing in your room, if you are daydreaming or when you are walking down the street listening or talking to your device or messaging. Simply  having your head down means that you are unaware and cannot see what is going on around you. If you are in code white then it will be very hard for you to notice anything bad or dangerous until it is too late. **

Code Yellow

Code yellow is the state of being aware. It is the code we should be in most of the time. You are relaxed but switched on to what is going on around you. Code yellow helps us see a problem before it happens, so that we can do something about it before things get worse. This does  not mean that you cannot listen to your headphones, talk on your phone or read a book, but you have an aware mind and are sensible about when and where you do these things.

Code Orange

Code orange is when you see a possible threat. This is when you see something that might be a problem. We go to code orange when something changes. For example, you might be walking down the

street and somebody steps out in front of you. You do not know they are a threat yet because they haven't said anything or made any action to show that they are a danger to you. However, you do know that your situation has changed so you are ready for anything.

Code Red

Code red is when there is a confirmed threat. This is when you are sure something is wrong and you must do something about it. This might be if a person steps in front of you and demands money from you, or tries to scare you, or your "gut" tells you that he is going to attack (see the previous chapter for possible signals).

If we are in code white, we will probably end up in code red without having time to be aware or see a possible threat. That is why we should mainly be in code yellow. We must always be aware so that we can switch to code orange if something changes and have time to deal with it. However, we cannot be in code orange all the time or we would be stressed out and hyperaware.

Here is a table to help you remember the awareness codes.

What colour?	What does it mean?	What do I need to do?
White	Relaxed and unaware - switched off	You won't know.
Yellow	Relaxed and aware, alert or switched on	You shouldn't need to do anything but you can if something happens
Orange	Possible threat	Be ready to act. Set your boundaries (see next chapter)
Red	Threat	Talk, shout, escape or fight

Hyperaware

Being hyperaware or paranoid is when you are extremely worried about people in general. This is not awareness. Being hyperaware means that you are being scared when you do not need to be. You are not listening to your instincts. What you are listening to is your imagination. Being paranoid can be just as bad as being unaware. This is because you are so worried about what might happen that you cannot concentrate on what is actually going on around you. It is also not very healthy and you will turn yourself into a nervous wreck, and you could make yourself ill.

If you are aware, you should be confident and relaxed because you understand what is going on at this particular moment in time. Most of the time nothing bad happens, but you can see and hear if it does and have enough time to do something about it. Here is a common everyday situation that shows you the difference between being unaware, hyperaware and aware.

You are about to cross the road.

- **Unaware**: You walk onto the road with your head down and without looking either side of you.
- **Hyperaware**: You are too scared to cross the road.
- **Aware**: You look both ways before crossing.

Likewise, in self-protection, an unaware person does not think that anyone will attack them; a hyperaware person thinks everyone might want to attack them; and an aware person knows that some people might attack them but that most people are okay.

Situational Awareness

Your awareness will change depending on your situation. Now, I know you will probably be sick of hearing adults (usually school teachers and often parents) telling you to "Pay attention", but that is really what awareness is all about. However, when it comes to self-protection, the attention you need to pay is to what is going on around you. This is a good way to understand code yellow. Pay attention to these five elements: **people, places, hazards, changes and context.**

- **People:** What types of people are present in your situation? Do you know most of them very well? Are they friendly? Do they make you feel nervous? Is there any one individual you feel might be a possible threat?
- **Places:** What do you know about the place you are in? Does it look dangerous? Does it have a bad reputation? Is it easy to get lost? Is it easy to get cornered? Where are the exits? Where do the exits lead?

- **Hazards:** If something bad happened what is likely to trip you up or get in your way should you have to make an exit? Is there anything in the room that might be used as a weapon?

- **Changes:** Any of the three previous elements are subject to change and can transform a non-dangerous situation into a threatening one. New people enter the environment that behave in a manner that makes you feel uneasy or perhaps someone who hasn't seemed to be threatening suddenly changes their mood. Depending on the time of day, an otherwise safe-looking place might become dangerous or, at least, quite different to what you usually expect. For example, a school in the day is quite a different place than when a disco is being held there at night. New hazards might present themselves such as when a glass is broken or a kettle is boiled. In the wrong hands, these can become new hazards for you.

- **Context:** What are the circumstances of your situation? Noisy and loud people at a party are in context because that is what is expected. However, noisy and loud people in a library or a cinema might be trouble. Long coats on a cold or windy day are normal but not on a hot sunny day unless the individual has a particular health condition. Such clothing might be used to conceal weapons.

Online Awareness

Although someone online cannot immediately reach you, it doesn't mean you don't have to be careful. Don't put online where you intend to go or where you visit regularly, especially if you are going there alone or without an adult present. Remember, unless you have met someone offline in the real world, you really don't know them. Some people go to great lengths to create a fantasy identity online and they can be very good at doing this for the express purpose of trapping victims. Be switched on when you turn to the virtual world.

** This isn't to say there won't be times even the best trained people will switch off. For example, you cannot really be in anything but code white when you go to sleep or when you have to totally focus on something. In such circumstances it is important to ensure you are totally secure first before you unwind. Code white should be carefully planned for such times and moments only.

The Fence - Setting Boundaries

Imagine you had a castle and you wanted to protect that castle from being invaded. What would you do? What have people done in the past? They have dug moats around the outside making it difficult to get into and they have stationed guards to defend the entrance. The line that is defended is called a boundary.

A boundary is a line that divides something or someone from everything else. People set all sorts of boundaries in life. For example, the boundary line between two houses makes it clear to the separate owners where their property ends and their neighbour's property begins. Boundaries might also be used to set how we allow another person to treat us. When someone says that another person has "crossed a boundary" they are usually describing behaviour they believe to be inappropriate. Perhaps this boundary-crosser has shared personal information without permission or maybe they made physical contact that made the first person feel uncomfortable.

We often set different boundaries for different people. Perhaps you have a relative, such as a grandparent or an aunt or uncle, who does not live with you but is given a key to your house. They can use the key in certain instances, but this key is not to be used outside of those circumstances or by anyone else. That is a personal security boundary set around certain members of your family. You and your family allow people to visit the house but that doesn't mean they can enter it whenever they please. Similarly, you probably have personal things you only want certain people, such as your close family, to know about you. That's a personal boundary you and those who have told have agreed to set.

The boundaries are the dividing lines we all set and we all should respect. However, they need protecting.

To this day, people protect boundaries outside buildings they own. You will see walls around factories and houses everywhere you go. One of the most common forms of boundary protection is a fence - you might have one around your house. We use it to protect the line we have drawn between our property and someone else's. This is also the name a top self-protection instructor, Geoff Thompson, gave to a very important self-protection idea.

The Idea of the Fence

The fence is anything that protects your personal space. You only allow people into your personal space that you trust. To see what your personal space is, stretch out your arm out in front of you and point your finger. Now draw an imaginary circle around you. This circle is your boundary line, which you will control with your fence. A common way of using the fence in self-protection is by using your hands. If you were to approach someone and they raised their arm

out towards you with the palm flat you would know that was the sign for "STOP!" It is a gesture respected all over the world and a very simple way to demonstrate how the self-protection fence works.

THE FENCE – SETTING BOUNDARIES

There are several ways we can create a fence with our hands when trying to make sure our personal boundaries are respected. These can vary depending on whom we are interacting with, but the aim is always to help you be in control of a situation. The following are different ways to create a fence between you and someone else.

Talking Hands

Try talking with your hands or keeping your hands in front of you when you talk to people. This is something that many public speakers and television presenters do in order help express themselves. We can use this behaviour to judge whether someone wants to hurt us and to give us a type of self-protection fence. You should try to make "talking hands" appear natural. Do not try to think about it too much, just make it part of the way you talk. The plan is not to make it artificial. If you think about it too much, you might take your attention off the possible threat or they might suspect you are adopting a protective position. If the possible threat does guess what you are doing then you will have to keep it up … but it is much better if they do not "see" your fence.

Lower Fences

Some people do not feel comfortable talking with their hands and do not feel natural doing it. That is fine. If you are one of these people, try holding your hands in front clasped together as your natural resting posture and then raise them (or just one of them) gently but firmly every time someone tries to get to close to you. Maybe you would prefer to cross your arms. This can also be an effective type of fence if done correctly. When you do this, do not tuck in your hand but have your weaker hand ready to show where your boundary lies and how far you will allow the other person to move forward. After the other person has stopped and doesn't move forward or steps back, this hand can then go back to either resting on your stronger side upper arm or maybe on your chin.

If this is not comfortable then carry your hands however you normally do but be ready to put one or both of your hands up when you see that someone is moving into your personal space. The further down and away your hands are (such as by your sides or behind your back) the harder it will be for you to establish your fence quickly as you will have to guess when someone is getting too close.

Fences Against Larger or Taller People

When someone is much bigger than you - such as an adult or a large teenager - we have to allow for more room because they have a longer reach. I would advise that you put a hand up as soon as you feel like someone might invade your personal space.

Remember: one hand forward with the palm out is the international sign for "STOP!" People instinctively know this and someone who doesn't want to get physical or hurt you will do  just that when you put your hand up.

THE FENCE – SETTING BOUNDARIES

Offsetting

You can offset someone using the fence by not facing them head-on, but moving on a 45-degree angle from the centre line of a possible attacker. Such a position places you to the side of the person. This puts you more in control because you can use both your arms, but he or she cannot reach you properly with one of theirs without changing their position to match yours. You can keep on offsetting someone by carefully moving from one 45-degree angle to another as you talk. Sometimes, just by doing this, you can change someone's mind about being aggressive to you because in the back of their head they feel less confident in the situation.

Practising

The only way you are going to be able to use the fence (or any physical skill for that matter) is by practising it regularly and making it a natural habit. First of all get used to your personal space. Draw your imaginary circle and see if you can control who comes into it and who does not. This can be done with friends and family but do not tell them you are doing it when you are practising. We are trying to train the behaviour so it becomes natural to you. You should never look like you are taking on a fighting pose. One simple way I teach the fence is to imagine you have to stand-up to give a talk to a classroom or that you are presenting a video. You will notice that professional people who do this when standing, such as teachers, television and video presenters, will stand with their feet balanced and will use their hands in a comfortable, easy manner. As I said before, the fence should always be natural and the best way to do this is to do it all the time.

Testing the Fence

An important part of anything you are practising is to test out your progress. Developing your ability to create and maintain a fence is no different. Here is a simple game to test the fence.

Get someone you trust to shout and insult you. Encourage them to try to make you walk backward or draw you out of your imaginary circle *without* making contact with you. You decide how personal you make the insults, but the more realistic the better. Just remember to both agree from the start that this is just a game. Set a time limit - for example two minutes. Here are the rules:

- They are not allowed to touch you in any way.
- If they move quickly into your space before you put your arms up, you have lost.
- If you back away as they move forward, you have lost.
- If you follow them as they back off, you have lost.
- You win if you keep them out of your space by using your fence for the set time.

All the time you are using the fence, try to keep calm. Remember the points from earlier in this book: try not to answer their insults or their aggressive questions. Just keep saying words like "No" calmly but firmly or give them instructions like "Stay where you are". Try changing the subject or just being nice. It will be hard to do, but the important thing is you are keeping them out of your space. No matter what they say and no matter what they call you, they have lost if you do not allow them in your space.

Angry Fence

This method is more physical than what we have discussed so far. The "anger" isn't real anger but the image of anger used to keep a would-be attacker away from you. It is also best used on people around your size and not on much bigger people. If someone gets into your personal space too quickly, and you know you are in danger, you need to make space as quickly as possible. A good way to do this is by using a sharp and powerful shove to their chest and then making one short shift back. Remember, this should only be done once. If your attacker enters your personal space more than once you will either run out of space to shift back to or it will just turn into a shoving competition and, if they are bigger than you, they will probably grab you.

As you shove and shift, use your voice. Try the words "Back off!" or "No!" or "Stay away!" Give these commands straight at the person you are shoving. What you have done is create distance. You have created a gap between you and your possible attacker. The shove and the shout will have shocked them a bit and they should be having second thoughts about whether to attack you or not. Two things have changed for them: they will have to cover that distance you have just created and you are not the easy prey they thought you were.

However, these thoughts might disappear if you do nothing else after the shove and the shout. You need to back it up quickly. As soon as you have shoved and shouted, point at the attacker. Continue shouting instructions to them: "Stay where you are!" You might also try pacing with your eyes fixed on them - like a tiger stalking its prey. These words and actions should make the person who wanted to hurt you feel like he is the one being attacked now. He or she might yell back at you - they probably will - and say plenty of "brave" words, but if they do not walk into your space they are not a threat. Being able to keep this distance by using your voice and actions, so that you can then slowly move away, takes a lot of **Courage** and **Discipline**, not to mention **Respect** for your abilities. However, you can do it if you practise and you are serious with your words and actions.

Remember, the anger you use is a weapon. The words and actions you use are done to protect your body from harm. If the situation does not get physical and you are able to walk away afterwards then the anger has done its job. Another important thing to remember is that the anger should stay behind in the place where you defended yourself and you can go on being happy with your life.

Reverse Angry Fence

Sometimes if a person gets into your space faster than you can erect your fence, they might shove you first. If this happens, it does not necessarily mean a fight has started. You can use the space given by the would-be attacker to stop the fight from happening. By raising your hands and taking a crouched position, you can make it clear that you do not want to fight. Many angry would-be attackers or bullies who feel they want to show their strength will feel that they don't need to do anything else. Of course, if the would-be attacker moves forward anyway your hands and body are in a strong position to fight back. This version of the angry fence requires a lot of **Courage** but it can be extremely useful.

Respecting Boundaries

Setting boundaries and understanding the boundaries of others is about Respect. This section has mostly talked about physical protection, but boundaries can also be set to keep our self-respect. For example, you might also use your boundary to decide the difference between what you believe to be right and what you believe to be wrong. If you feel that something is wrong you should not "go along" with it but keep behind your boundary. We should also set an example to others by respecting other people's boundaries. Think about this the next time you try to convince someone to do something they don't want to do. By demonstrating a strong willingness to respect the word "no" helps create a healthy understanding of one another's boundaries.

Dealing with a Physical Situation

As we have discussed before, self-protection is largely about stopping a physical situation from happening. However, if it does happen we need to know what to do and how to do it. This is what we call *self-defence.*

The Three Ps

All good self-defence training revolves around **pre-emption**, **proactivity** and **pressure testing**. Pre-emption is the act of doing something before someone else does. This is also being proactive but proactivity also covers continuing to stay in charge a situation and not to wait for someone else to take action. As soon as we act against a threat, we need to keep pressing forward until we can escape. Pressure testing means that all our physical skills and training in self-defence must be tried out against training partners who resist. This can take the form of games or various other activities. It is fine and expected that you will fail during your training; this is all part of learning and helps you see how much you are improving.

Tactical Escape

Of our body's two most basic survival actions - flight (run) or fight - flight is the stronger. This is what we are always aiming for in a self-protection situation. We want to escape the situation by either avoiding it in the first place by using our **Awareness,** or by using our voice, or by escaping.

Here are few things to remember before you start training tactical escape exercises and games:

- Do not just blindly run. If you just run away from someone without any idea of where you are trying to run you can end up in many different problems. Firstly, your pursuer might catch up with you if they are a faster runner. Secondly, if you don't know the area you are running in or you aren't concentrating, you might end up running down a dead end. In short, think **run towards safety** rather than simply running away from danger.

- Know where your exits are in any given place, whether you are inside or outside. These should take you to an area you are most likely to be safe.

- Check for obstructions between you and the nearest exit.

When being pursued look for objects that can be used as shields or as means to obstruct your pursuer.

- When in a room it is usually best to have your back towards a wall. That way you keep your eyes on everything that is going on at all times whilst limiting the chances of another person or a hazard surprising you from behind.

- When in a large open space, where you will have to run a longer distance, you will need to be facing away from your threat but learn to run in a zigzag. This makes pursuing you more difficult.

- Always look for objects you can use to move behind or to get between you and your pursuer. Be careful not to choose anything that will get you trapped. Assessing obstacles, along with your exits, should all be part of your regular awareness as you scan your surroundings.

DEALING WITH A PHIYSCAL SITUATION

Practical Exercises

Escape Only Activities

Exit!

- Whilst you are taking part in an activity, have someone call "Exit!"

- These commands should be done without warning and when you are in the middle of doing something else. This is to speed up your reactions.
- Remember to have your back to exits when you are inside and to zigzag run when you are outside or in especially large spaces.

Obstacle & Agility Training

- Use agility equipment such as ladders and cones to improve your ability to move quickly. There are many different agility cone and ladder exercises that will keep you nimble on your feet. Try different movement patterns and position the cones and ladders near exit points.
- Use obstacle courses. Create your own (ensure they are safe by arranging them with responsible adults) or use readymade ones. This sort of training keeps you agile and thinking when you are on the move. Once you get used to running the obstacle course, arrange games using them, or chase/race other people through them.

Chasing Games

Because most attackers are bigger than you, there is one major advantage on your side: agility. Your size makes it easier to avoid them. A good game to test this is Build-up Tag (some people call it "Bulldogs"). Here are the rules to our version of the game.

- One person is "It". Their job is to tag all the other people.
- When you are caught you join his or her side and try to catch anyone who has not been caught.
- You either play the game with two three-second bases or no bases at all. A base is a place decided upon where It cannot tag you.
- Three-second bases mean that as soon as an un-tagged person reaches them they only have three seconds to stay there before they have to run to the second one. It is good to have a referee who counts when everyone reaches the base.
- The winner is the last person who has not been tagged.

Weapon Awareness Game

Another type of chasing game is something we call "Weapon Awareness". You will need a safe small object as a pretend weapon for this game, such as a collapsible, disposable drinking bottle. You will also need a fairly large group of friends to practise with.

- There needs to be two sides. The bigger side are the normal people who do not have weapons. The smaller side have one or more of the practise/toy weapons on them.
- The smaller side hide the practise/toy weapon and mingle with the other side
- Players on the smaller side decide when to pull the practise/toy weapon on a player from the other side and try to make contact with the person by touching them with the practise/toy weapon
- As soon as a player from the bigger side sees a weapon they should shout "Knife!" or "Weapon!" or "He/she's got a weapon!" and move to an exit
- The exits in the game must be real exits
- This can be a fun game, but remember how you train is how you will act in real life so take it seriously with the shouting and the escaping
- Do not immediately run back into the play area: only do this when that game is over

You can vary this game by just having one practise/toy weapon hidden on a person on the small side. This is very good for practising your observation skills.

Weapon Awareness Game - Partner Version

You can play the weapon awareness game with just two people. The person who is "armed" with the practise/toy weapon can hide it in different places as he/she approaches his/her partner who can be stood with their back against the wall. This is good for practising your fence and for improving your confidence. You can practise alerting people by shouting "Show me your hands!" if you see them hide one hand behind their back or hold it in a suspicious way as they approach you.

Striking and Escaping from the Fence

Sadly, sometimes things will get physical and if this happens you must keep control of the situation. In real life, striking someone is likely to cause injury to your attacker and maybe to you. If you strike another child, you could get yourself into a lot of trouble. This is why we do our best to avoid hitting someone for real, but if someone is a physical threat and comes into your space then this might be your only option.

Remember, self-defence is your right but it ceases to become self-defence if it cannot be justified. Self-defence is the use of physical force to prevent or stop a crime from happening. Revenge and retaliation are not self-defence. Attacking someone just because they hurt your feelings is not self-defence, even if you think they deserve it. Self-defence is not about revenge and it is not retaliation. In short: you need to be able to say that you used force to stop someone from *immediately* hurting you or someone else.

The man has a longer range, making the girl set her fence further out. His head is not an easy target.   *The girl targets his hand as he tries to reach for her.*   *She runs away from the direction she has struck the hand.*

If you see striking as your only option, you will have to do it very hard, probably several times and very quickly … but only do it so you can escape. Do not wait and try to block their strike first; it is very unlikely you will have time or be able to predict exactly when they will strike.

We can strike with our hands, elbows, head, knees or feet. Aim at a suitable target around your head height. Attack anything you can reach if you can't get the best targets. If the person has a much longer reach than you, strikes are probably best aimed at their hands and you should escape to the outside of the shoulder of the hand you have struck.

If a threatening person touches your fence or moves into your personal space and you do not have time to shove them, you will have to strike them in self-defence. A good way to practise this is for someone to hold a focus mitt (a boxer's punching pad) and to get them to step into your fence. You strike the pad with your palm or, if you are wearing a bag glove (gloves used for punching pads and bags), hit with a fist. If you want to use a fist, make sure you make a fist properly and safely with your fingers curled into our palm and your thumb across them. Don't tuck your thumb inside your fist.

It is best to practise this exercise with a good self-defence teacher who will teach you how to strike properly, however, here are few basics to keep in mind for striking from the fence for self-defence.

- When you strike, you will need to strike hard and until the target is no longer there and/or you can make your escape. **Remember** you only strike from the fence when someone touches it and you fear that they want to hurt you.
- Although striking hard is certainly important in self-defence, we all have to be careful that we do not injure ourselves or cause problems later on in life. Your bones will still be soft until you are at least 18 years of age. With this in mind, if your hands start hurting when you are practising your striking then stop immediately. Work on being accurate with your strikes and then build up your speed. If you do decide to punch, wear good quality hand-wraps (learn how to bandage

your hands like a boxer) and padded gloves under the supervision of a qualified teacher.

- Strike a target until the target is covered (for example, one focus mitt is placed over the other) and then quickly make your escape to the nearest exit point.

- Try using your fence with your back against the wall and with the person facing you. In a real situation, we should always seek escape. By putting yourself in this position you have to fight in order to escape. Another good reason to train this way is that you will learn to strike at close range where self-defence fights are likely to occur. Other benefits are that the wall will stop you pulling your arm back when you strike, making your strike less easy to see coming, and you will learn how to fight out of confined spaces..

- Strike from different angles. There are hundreds of different techniques that people can show you but really there are only two ways you can strike: in a straight line or on a curve. Practise both of these.

- Remember your attacker might be much larger than you, or even an adult, so you may need to imagine your fence further out. When training for this, you will have to think about striking hands rather than targets on the body so I would advise that you practise hitting the back of a gloved hand (see the images on the previous page).

- It is good to get used to striking from different positions. You might not always be standing up in a self-defence situation so we need to train for sitting, kneeling and even from our backs. This also makes you work harder and the training strengthens your strikes for when you are standing up again.

Safety note for pad holders: Always hold the pad firmly and never pull it away once someone is about to strike. If the striker hits the air or an unsupported pad full force they can injure their joints. Because the bodies of children under 18 years old are not fully developed it is good to get softer and thicker pads for them to strike. They should never punch the pad without the correct gloves and I would advise that they hit with open hands first. To make it more realistic, you should move backwards as the striker strikes and even turn on an angle as a real life target would after being struck.

Further Training

Learning when and how to strike from the fence is a very important skill, but it is also very important for you to test yourself safely yet honestly against someone who is not just holding a target. You can do this is in the types of games I teach on my courses and in my lessons, which you can find out about at the end of the book. Alternatively, I would advise that you do some sparring at your local boxing, wrestling or judo club. Rugby is also a very good sport for learning how to escape and also to prepare you for the rough and tumble of real situations.

Self-Defence Fighting

My courses and lessons teach many different physical exercises based on the chasing game and I also cover defensive fighting for when there are no other better options. However, in order to train this way safely you need to be practising under the  instruction of a good teacher and be using the correct equipment.

Therefore, I have decided not to include this part in the book. A future book may feature all the physical exercises that can be performed with mats and protective equipment. In the meantime, however, practise the exercises I have described in this chapter, the previous one and the following one. They will show how to judge if a situation is about to become physical, practise your escaping and avoidance skills, and - as described in the next chapter - **train to never give in!**

The Will to Survive

Train Hard; Fight Easy!

There is a proverb, dating back to the 1600s, which says, "Where there is a will, there is a way". Everyone has will and we all have a choice to keep our will or give up. Remember, in a real-life self-protection situation, your attacker will try to scare you into giving up and they might use pain to make you surrender. If there is one rule to remember in self-protection, it is "Never Give In". Changing your tactics is fine. *Pretending* to give in to your attacker is fine. However, you should never give up the main plan or strategy: get to safety.

Before we look at this last, yet very important, part of self-protection training, I wish to revise what we have already learnt and what should be understood up to this point of the book. If you are unsure about any of the points below please go back to previous chapters or look at the glossary at the end. Make sure you reread until you feel sure you understand.

- You know that using our instincts and being aware of our surroundings will mean that you have a better chance of seeing trouble before it happens - in other words you will know when to avoid something.
- You know that there is no point in being paranoid or hyperaware - scared of everything - as this is both bad for your health and not helpful for your self-protection, as you will miss the real threat.
- You know that having self-respect means that you will be prepared to do whatever you can to survive and having respect for others means that you will not bully or intentionally start trouble with others.
- You know that you need to keep your personal space only for those who you have good reason to trust. You know that the fence is used to let you know whether someone you don't trust wants to get physical.
- You know that self-protection is all about being in charge of yourself and controlling a situation. If you feel something is wrong you must act straight away rather than allow a possible threat to take control.
- You understand what to look out for in different types of attackers.
- You know about spotting con tricks or people who are trying to control you by deception.
- You understand how adrenaline affects our body.
- You know several different signs an aggressive person will show before they are about to attack.
- You know that if you have to fight to survive you have to take control as soon as possible and not wait to be attacked.

- You know that escape is the most important goal in self-protection.
- Finally you understand that real physical situations might mean that you will get hurt and hurt badly. This is when will really comes in…

Train Hard; Fight Easy

You have already decided that you are worth fighting for and that is what self-respect really means, but are you willing to put the work in? All the tenets of **Respect, Awareness, Courage, Discipline** and **Open Mind** are required when you work to develop will - the will to survive!

I believe your life and health are worth the biggest of fights, but you need to believe this as well. Try saying, "I am worth fighting for and I won't stop until I am safe". Keep this in mind as your physical training gets harder and harder. The great 18th century Russian general Count Alexander Suvorov is credited with the famous proverb, "Train hard; fight easy". Suvorov suggested that the more you push yourself in your training then the better your chances should be in real life, particularly if things go bad. Do not listen to people who say things like "But in real life I would fight harder" or "In real life I wouldn't give up" when it is pretty obvious that they give up when anything gets hard. All our self-protection training in this book has been about creating behaviours. Behaviours are learned through regular use. So think about this every time you feel bored with your physical training, every time you feel tempted to mess around in class or to skip it altogether and, most importantly, every time you feel like giving in!

Testing your Will

Your will is tested when you have to make a decision whether to go training or to play outside on a sunny day. Your will is tested when you have to make a decision to go training or watch that exciting new programme, film or video that has just premiered. One thing I will promise you is that if you train as hard as you can and keep on testing your will in training then when you do go outside in the sun or watch that show or even drink a glass of water … you will enjoy it a hundred times more. Good training, when you feel you have pushed yourself and tested your will, teaches you the meaning of the word "treat"!

When you train, you need to push yourself in at least one activity. Not everything you train needs to be exhausting but everything you train is worth doing well. Nothing should be done half-heartedly. Remember, in a real-life physical situation there is no time to be half-hearted about anything and everything has to be done with maximum effort. Half-heartedness in real-life could cost you your life. Of course, training will be tough and uncomfortable. We are not like our ancestors who had to fight to survive every day, so it is very natural for us to want to take the easy path and be comfortable. However, when you are uncomfortable you grow because you teach yourself to be stronger in the mind and in the body. You are training for a worst-case situation and in order to do that you need to have a stronger will than your attacker. This is what people mean when they talk about having "fighting spirit" or a "warrior's heart".

Practical

Anything that makes you tired very quickly is a good "Will Drill". You should train hard in all your practical activities and remember if you are not sweating and breathing hard at the end of a session then you haven't got the most out of that lesson. There should be one exercise each week that you nominate the "Will Drill". This should be the exercise where you push yourself so hard that you want to give up, but you keep going until it is impossible to do anymore. If you are fortunate enough to have a teacher that trains practical self-defence then you will have the opportunity to use skills that are directly connected to the material covered in this book. For example, your Will Drill might be to repeatedly escape out of a corner against one or more training partners who play the role of your attacker or attackers. This exercise becomes a Will Drill when you start feeling the urge to just let them smother you and have to go deep inside your mind to say "No, I will escape!"

All sparring in boxing, Thai boxing, wrestling, judo, Brazilian jiu jitsu and self-defence clubs is good for testing your will. In the grappling arts (Brazilian jiu jitsu, judo and wrestling) try fighting whilst someone is pinning you down to test your will. You will be amazed that if you keep on going you will discover even the biggest people make mistakes and you will escape.

Just like in self-defence, you should use your will in all that you do. At school always try your very hardest at P.E. or sports. For example, don't just walk at cross-country but try to run or jog all the way, even if you have to change your speed. Remember, running is an important part of self-protection and there was even an entire French martial art based on escape called Parkour (which we now know as the incredible and dangerous stunt art of "Free Running").

Will Drills might often be physical but the real strength they are testing is mental strength. We are trying to make our minds tough and resilient.

Even in our non-physical education we can use our will. Sometimes when we get a boring subject to study for our homework it takes a lot of will and a lot of **Discipline** to try our best. Remember, the secret to growing is to always be better than we were before. That is how our bodies naturally work as we grow up so that is how our will, fitness and mind need to develop as well. However, they won't grow strong if you settle for half-heartedness.

Safety Note
Those suffering from asthma or other conditions that affect breathing or respiration should keep their inhaler at hand at all times and use it whenever it is necessary. Always speak to a Doctor before

you take up any physical activity. You can always work around illness, health problems or injuries, but you will need to be careful not to make your condition any worse. This will mean picking exercises that will test you and be challenging but will not put your health in danger. Discuss it with your parents, your instructor and your local Doctor.

So, before we move onto our final chapter let us look at will through the tenets:

Respect: We gain more self-respect through working harder and pushing ourselves never to give up. We know how much hard work we have put into our training and know that we deserve to live the best life that we can make for ourselves.

Awareness: Through training very hard, we become more aware of ourselves and just how far we can go. We become aware of some incredible possibilities. We also understand just how far others can go.

Courage: Remember, courage is a matter of choice. When we are training or testing our will, we make a choice. It is up to us to decide to take that class, to choose the hard activity and to push ourselves as far as possible. Courage in this chapter is all about fighting our fear of hard work.

Discipline: This is very important when it comes to will. Your self-discipline is also a choice and it gets stronger the more you test your will. Discipline here is to remember that you need to do Will Drills regularly. If you keep at something and you push yourself to get better - even only a little better - each time, you will amaze yourself when you look back at how you used to be and how much better you have become.

Open Mind: Your mind becomes open to what you are capable of when you push yourself on a regular basis. You start to realize that if you can achieve one thing and get results from that, you can achieve loads of things.

What Happens Afterwards

We have mainly been discussing how to avoid, reduce and manage a potentially violent situation. Such circumstances are naturally stressful. How we respond to these stressful feelings can have a large impact on what happens after a violent or potentially violent episode. In this chapter, I am going to teach you about how to manage yourself after you have dealt with a possible or an actual self-protection threat.

Stay Alert

Just because one bad thing is seemingly over it doesn't mean you are out of danger. You should go back to code orange immediately afterwards, being observant of other dangers. A tactical escape doesn't end with you getting away from the threat. You need to be switched onto other hazards such as traffic, other people or obstacles that could injure you because you are only focused on fleeing from one dangerous situation. Know where you are headed for safety and only begin to relax once you have arrived at this place.

Often, if you feel you have done a good job in stopping a violent situation, you will feel a pleasant sensation flood your body. Think of a time when you were really worried or perhaps had lost a really important item, only to have the problem resolved and all your worries washed away. This is the same feeling you will experience if you think you have done a good job at stopping a threat. Your body is rewarding you for doing the right thing to survive and helping to bring your heart rate down. However, you need to be wary of this feeling immediately after the situation has past. Take a breath and stay alert. It's not over until you are sure you are in a safe place.

WHEN PARENTS AREN'T AROUND:
A YOUNG PERSON'S GUIDE TO SELF-PROTECTION

First Aid

When your body is in stress, the brain releases what is sometimes called a "chemical cocktail". These are naturally occurring chemicals used to help us when we are in fight or flight mode, and they include endorphins: the body's natural painkiller. After an incident we may realise we have been injured but not picked up on it at the time due to the pain-numbing effects of these chemicals. Therefore, it is very important to do an immediate body check as soon as you are in a position of safety. This body-check should be built into your physical training. You might notice that you also feel other sensations: a feeling of being hot or cold, a tingling sensation, or a feeling of breathlessness and light-headedness. These are all natural responses of the body to stress. Continue to take controlled breaths and, if necessary, "ground" yourself by holding onto something solid.

I highly recommend that you complete a First Aid course as part of your self-protection training. There are age-appropriate courses you can do and will provide training in how to handle medical emergencies. This is important for you or anyone who may be hurt in a violent situation or an accident.

As with any violent situation, it is also important to be able to report a medical emergency to a responsible person. This might take the form of the emergency services.

Reporting

After a violent or potentially violent situation it is very important you speak to someone responsible. This someone should be an adult you can trust, such as a parent. If the incident has occurred at school, it will probably be a member of staff, such as a teacher. Depending on the seriousness of a situation, you might need to make an official report to someone in authority. In some cases, if it is particularly serious, the police might need to be informed. It is very important that you give yourself time before making such a report. Never be rushed into making this type of report or saying anything other than someone attacked you or tried to attack you. Your emotions will be high and it is important that you give yourself time to calm down before you properly talk about this incident. You need to get your thoughts together so that you can be factual in your full report. This type of reporting must be done with a responsible and trusted adult present. This is the same whether you give your report in verbal or written form.

Aftermath

Later on, after the event, you might get an overflow of emotions that could take the form of anger, uncontrollable crying, over-sensitivity or fear. You might get a combination of all these feelings. You might also feel numb for a while. This is all part of the "aftermath" and how we cope with coming to terms with a crisis after it has happened. Understand that this is natural and all part of the process of how human beings deal with intense situations. Remember, each person's aftermath is different – including how long it can last for. Don't hesitate in asking for some time out from whatever you are doing in order to cope or asking for professional help. There are trained counsellors at school or privately outside of school that you can talk to about your experience and how you are feeling. It is important that you do not try to fight against these feelings but remember to breathe, to talk when you need to and to take your time.

The Black Dog & "Should Have"

The Black Dog is the name given to what is often referred to as depression. Whilst everyone experiences periods of depression (or low moods) to a certain degree, Clinical Depression is a serious condition that affects patients on a regular basis. If you are finding that you are feeling upset long after a violent incident, it would be useful to speak to a doctor. It is important to have any long-term effect diagnosed by a professional and to get help.

When we think of the Black Dog in self-protection, we are usually discussing the mental torture many of us put ourselves through at the thought of what we should have done. If you are safe, you did the right thing. Understand that it is only natural to doubt yourself afterwards, this is part of the way we learn about experiences and prepare for the future, but in doing so you need to remember that we cannot change the past. The most important thing for you is that you are safe. Don't be persuaded by others who weren't in your situation and may want to make you feel bad about what you did or didn't do. If you are practising good self-protection then you did everything in your ability to avoid a violent situation, including walking away from a fight challenge or, if you had to fight, it was to stop someone hurting you or another. Don't let the Black Dog follow you. Let that shadowy canine loose to bark at the darkness and away from you

When Parents *are* Around: Children and Parents Training Together

There is plenty a child and an adult can do together to help improve self-protection. The first thing you can do is make sure that at least one of your parents or your guardian reads this book - even better, try reading it together. Then ask your parents to help test you with your self-protection exercises. Simple exercises can be chasing exercises or holding the focus mitts (striking pads). They can also help with the various fence tests. However, the best exercises parents can do with you are ones that you can do in everyday life.

Awareness Exercises

When you go for a walk with your parents or are sitting in the car or on a bus, tell them what you see around you. Listen to your "gut" and describe which people you would approach in an emergency and which people you feel you should avoid. Also get used to spotting different places: what places you could use as a "safe base" and what places you feel are not safe.

Purpose: You will become more aware of your surroundings and will be able to spot both safety and danger better.

Search Exercise

When you are in a supermarket or a big shop, ask your parents to watch you as you ask strangers where to find certain things. After you have finished shopping, tell your parents why you chose each person.

Purpose: This will help you recognise who are trustworthy people you can ask. You will be amazed at what your "gut" tells you about people.

Making a Pledge

Your parents (or your guardian) care about you more than anyone else in the world. The fact that they have probably bought this book for you shows that they really love you and want to protect you. It is only right that you show them you are willing to protect yourself. The more you demonstrate to them that you are capable of looking after yourself in certain situations and will be mindful of your safety, the more likely they are to worry less and allow you to do more in life. Furthermore, if you become involved in a serious fight they will know that your actions were only in self-defence.

People have often made pledges, vows, and oaths to show they are being honest. It is a demonstration of their loyalty. The pledge I would like you make is one that will let your parents know that you are serious about protecting yourself.

You can either say it to them or, if you like, write it down on a piece of paper (you might even want to design it to look like a certificate that you both sign). Say it or write it how you want so long as you make the following honest promises:

- Promise that you will always tell your parents where you are going if you leave your home by yourself.
- Promise that if you are ever involved in a serious fight, it will only be to protect yourself and that you have done everything you can to stop it from happening.

WHEN PARENTS *ARE* AROUND: CHILDREN AND PARENTS TRAINING TOGETHER

This way you can work with your parents and they can trust that you understand what it is meant by self-protection.

WHEN PARENTS AREN'T AROUND:
A YOUNG PERSON'S GUIDE TO SELF-PROTECTION

Questions & Answers on

Self-Protection

Q. Isn't self-protection all about fighting?

No, self-protection is about keeping safe and doing what is needed to keep you away from serious danger. You only fight when there is no other way you can make your escape.

Q. Doesn't self-protection mean you have to wait for someone to attack before you do anything?

In real life, if you are switched on and are aware of your personal space you will know when someone wants to physically attack you because they will try to get across your "fence". When they do this, you should act before they can hit or grab you.

Q. Will taking up a martial art help me to defend myself?

There are many different schools of martial arts all teaching very different things. It is true that there are useful things you can take from the various martial arts to help you with your self-protection training, but always remember to keep things simple; and it is always best to talk down or use your voice in a real situation. When it comes to the physical side of things the following types of training are best avoided in self-protection:

- Any training where you wait for someone to do something physical to you before you do anything i.e. you have to wait to block their strike or grab you. This doesn't mean you shouldn't train for when someone has already acted – you should have good recovery options – but the training should not rely on this as the main strategy.

- Any training that is complicated. In real-life it is unlikely that you will be able to remember complicated combinations when put under extreme pressure.
- Any training that seems to lack any form of pressure testing. For example: where the whole lesson seems to be about people letting you do things to them without ever testing if it really works.

Good sports that will help you improve your physical skills include boxing, wrestling, judo, Brazilian jiu jitsu, Thai boxing, American football or rugby. Also, don't forget running and playing tag or tig! However, remember that they are all sports and in real life you are more interested in survival than winning and the chances are you won't be dealing with someone who is training in the same activity as you. This means they won't always do what another player might do and they certainly won't be playing by the rules of the sport.

Q. How am I supposed to remember my self-protection training in a real-life situation?

This is perhaps one of the best questions you can ask. And the best answer is to practise self-protection all the time. Don't think that you will suddenly be able to "do self-protection" if it is not something that comes naturally to you. Make it a part of your everyday life. Be mindful of your personal space and others. Assess where you are at all times: taking into account what people are present and what you know about them; the time of day; possible hazards; and if something changes.

QUESTIONS & ANSWERS ON SELF-PROTECTION

This applies just as much online, such as in the virtual world of gaming or through social media, as it does offline and in the "real world". Being "switched on" is not just about being able to spot an attacker but also being aware of other dangers. Most of us do a type of self-protection anyway. For example, we brush our teeth at night and in the morning to protect them from gum disease and tooth decay and we fasten our seatbelts so that we are better protected if our car is involved in an accident. Likewise, we should be aware of our personal space at all times and be aware what is going on around us. Training the physical side also has the extra benefit of keeping our bodies healthy so we can live longer and happier lives.

Q. What about "Special Moves"?

So-called "special moves" only work in fantasy fiction such as stories, TV shows, movies and games. In short, they are made-up and do not exist in real life. You can never rely on anything that is not tested under pressure and does not come naturally to you. The more incredible or flashy the move seems, the less likely it will work in a real-life situation. From time to time, you will see someone pull off an amazing spinning or acrobatic move against a genuine opponent but these are exceptional circumstances.

In reality, even the dead simple stuff that you have worked on again and again, and under pressure, will never be guaranteed to work. It will only give you more of a chance than you had before. No one but you will know how you will act in a real-life situation and even then, you will only find out when it happens to you. This is why it is important to train the physical stuff in a safe environment, under an experienced teacher and under some real honest pressure. Do not be fooled by people who can seemingly control, knock over or knock out people with little or no contact. This is a form of trickery that only works between teachers and their students who are either acting or have bought into the fantastical idea. These types of moves have never been proven to work when put under genuine pressure or scientific conditions.

Q. Won't Self-Protection make me more violent?

If you have read this book properly you will see that it is mainly about avoiding violence and even when you have to fight, you do it to escape and not to "win".

Q. Isn't there a risk of injury when I do the physical stuff?

There is risk that you might be hurt when you train in self-protection, but you will find that you are more at risk from serious injury when you are riding your bike or going ice-skating than you are from training in the toughest of self-protection clubs. Just make sure that a qualified instructor runs your club. Your parents should check that he or she has a clean DBS form (Disclosure and Barring Service), a First Aid certificate, is fully insured and has a teaching qualification under a reputable self-protection and/or martial arts governing body. In fact, parents should watch lessons as often as possible to see what they can do to help their children improve. It is true that the physical stuff will have a lot of "rough and tumble" and, as with all contact activities such as football, hockey and rugby, tears are not uncommon. In self-protection this is because training for the worse case situations is not comfortable. However, it is very rare that you will get anything more than the occasional bruise or cut.

Q. What about Stranger Danger?

Stranger Danger was an easy way to teach children not to go with people they did not know. This is still good advice but it is also important to remember that, sometimes, you might need a stranger to help you. Keep your distance from anyone you don't trust or any person who has done something that has given you good reason not to trust them. Be wary of people you don't know *who choose to approach you* - most of the time they will be okay, but consider that by coming up to you, they have taken charge of the situation already. You must always stay in control, protect your personal space - remember it becomes larger when the person outside it has a longer reach than you - and listen to your "gut feeling". If someone tells you not to tell anyone about something that you are not comfortable about or know is wrong, especially if they threaten you (or threaten your friends or family), ignore them and tell your parents, schoolteachers or some other adult you can trust. This is always better and stops them from having control over you. A simple way to remember this rule is: If they say, "Don't tell" then Tell! And if they say, "Don't yell" then Yell!

Q. How do I get help if someone is trying attack me or is attacking me?

There is a centuries-old phrase, "There's safety in numbers". For the most part it is true. It is nearly always safer to be in a group of trusted people. Most attackers (muggers and other predators) are unlikely to commit a crime when there are lots of people around. This isn't to say that people don't get attacked when they are in a group or in crowded places. They certainly do but it is less common.

However, what is surprising to most of us is that, when attacks do occur, how many people stand around doing nothing or just film what is happening without offering help. There are lots of reasons put forward for this happening but it is not usually because people don't care. When there are more people in one place and no-one is leading them, many people freeze to await instructions. Once people start doing things and telling people what to do, they start acting. Most people care when you ask for help. We see this all the time when disasters happen. What you need to do in a bad situation is to recruit help from bystanders (people watching on) by looking them in the eye and telling them what to do: "Call the police", "Call a teacher", "Get him off me", "You two, grab his arms" and so on.

Q. Can't I just shout, "Help"? Some people say I should shout "Fire"

Making any noise is a good thing. However, just shouting, "Help" at no one in particular is not good for getting the attention of individuals and it doesn't give them any instructions. There is no evidence to support the advice that calling "Fire" is better than calling for "Help". Rather than doing either of these two things, look people in the eye and give them instructions. You can practise this in chase games where some people play the role of the predators and others the bystanders. It is even better if the bystanders are adults like your parents or self-protection teachers.

Glossary

Adrenaline

This is a hormone in your body that is produced when you are under stress. It is natural and everyone feels its effects when they are frightened or angry. It can make you feel stronger and fast for a very short period if you understand when it is affecting you. It can make you feel sick, make you need the toilet, and even make your legs shake. The way to handle it is by recognising the feeling and taking deep controlled breaths.

Avoidance

This is when we keep away from something we know could be dangerous. We should always do our best to avoid a dangerous situation. We can do this by being aware and not worrying what others will think.

Awareness

We should be aware at all times. This means that we know what is going on around us.

Biting

In a real fight there are no rules so you can bite but do not rely on this method. When you train just say, "Bite!" when your mouth is close to a target. This sort of training must only be done under the supervision of an experienced self-defence instructor.

WHEN PARENTS AREN'T AROUND:
A YOUNG PERSON'S GUIDE TO SELF-PROTECTION

Boundaries

The boundaries are the dividing lines we all set and we all should respect. However, they need protecting.

Bully

Anyone who picks on someone else, either physically or with words, to frighten him or her or make him or her do something they don't want to do or to simply make them feel bad.

Bystander

This is a person who watches an event or situation but does not act. In self-protection we try to get onlookers to be helpful by giving them clear, simple instructions.

Context

This is the circumstance that sets up a situation. Anything that is unusual and does not fit in with what you would expect in a situation is "out of context". For example, someone wearing a long coat on a hot day is out of context unless they have some obvious health issue.

Courage

This means being brave when you do what you know is right even though it might be scary or others might make fun of you. Remember, everyone gets frightened but the courageous people are those who face their fears when they have a good reason.

Discipline

This is more about self-discipline and learning (remember the word "discipline" comes from the same word that we derive "disciple"). We need to work hard at our training, keep a good respectful attitude in the outside world and not take easy shortcuts when we know they are wrong. Self-protection is all about putting you in control and helping you take charge of your life. If you do not have control over yourself then how can you hope to have control over a situation?

Escape

Our main goal in self-protection is escape. We can escape through getting away before anything happens. Even when we have to fight back, our main goal is to get away from our attacker or attackers.

Elbow Strikes

This is a close range defensive attack that can be very damaging. We can use focus mitts, "Thai pads" (a type of large focus mitts), kick shields and heavy bags to train these strikes. Elbows can be thrown in different directions but are best thrown straight for basic self-defence.

Fear

Fear is the emotion of being scared or frightened of something. We all have fears and we all get scared, even the toughest, bravest and nastiest of us. Fear is just a word we use to describe when our instincts warn us of something that might be dangerous. It is also used to describe the feeling we get from adrenaline when our body is getting ready to act in a stressful situation. There is good and bad fear. Good fear is when you are being warned about a real threat (see Instinct). Bad fear is when you let something that you are afraid of stop you from living the life that you want.

Fence, The

The fence can be anything you use to keep a potential threat away from you and out of your personal space. The most common fences in self-protection are your arms, which you should learn to use naturally to keep your distance and act when you sense someone making a move to invade your personal space. However, if your arms are not long enough then the fence might be an object you put in between you and a potential attacker or an imaginary point you set in front of your outstretched arms. You set your fence on an imaginary boundary line that you draw and understand that when someone crosses it you will have to act immediately.

Fighting

Real fighting only ever happens when something has gone wrong with your awareness. It means you haven't spotted the danger early enough. We fight when we need to survive and do just enough to escape. Match fighting, where two people decide to have a fight, should be restricted to sports.

Fist

The fist can be used in a punch or like a downward club. The hand should be closed with all the fingers rolled in and the thumb on the outside, tight across the fingers. You should only hit with your fists in training when wearing proper gloves (bag gloves for pads and sparring gloves for sparring and pressure testing) or hand-wraps/bandages.

Grappling

Grappling is another name for wrestling, but it is also used to describe all types of wrestling from judo to Olympic wrestling to folk wrestling. We grapple when things go wrong in a violent situation and striking isn't an available option or we use it for less dangerous situations, such as restraining someone. We usually use grappling training to get to a better position to strike or/and escape or for the great movement skills it teaches.

GLOSSARY

Groin

This is the target area between the legs for both males and females. It is not always easy to hit, but it is a good area to strike when trying to escape.

Ground-Fighting

Fighting whilst on the ground should be avoided in most self-defence situations but we should always train for what happens if we end up there. Our main goal, if we end up on the ground, is to get back to our feet.

Hyperaware

See paranoid.

Instinct

This is our "gut feeling". Instinct helps us read signs in a potentially threatening situation. We should always "listen" to our instinct if something could be dangerous.

Kicking

Kicks are strikes delivered with the shin or foot. They are best aimed low and as a back-up method after the hands. Good Thai boxing clubs are recommended to help you with your kicking. You should only train this under the instruction of a good martial arts or self-defence teacher. Kicks can be thrown straight, on a curve or as a stamp.

Knee Strikes

The largest joint of the body is used against targets when defending at close range. We can use focus mitts, "Thai Pads" (a type of large focus mitt), kick shields and belly pads, in addition to heavy bags, to train these strikes. Knee strikes can be thrown different ways but they are most effectively thrown straight forward (like a spear) or in an upward motion. The knee can also be used in grappling to pin from the top or as shield from the back.

Martial Arts

These are combat systems created for different reasons. Most are good for sport, health and art, but few are taught in a way to make them effective in defending you in the modern world. You can take certain things from different martial arts, but in the end it is down to *you* to make *you* effective.

Offsetting

This is when you get yourself in a good position when using the fence. It is usually at a 45-degree angle to the threat you are facing, so that you are no longer standing directly in front of a threat, and gives you an advantage should anything happen.

Open Mind

We keep our mind open so that we can learn more and we can change (adapt) if needed.

Orange, Code

This is a state of awareness whereby you notice that something has changed and you are getting yourself ready to deal with it if you need to. In code orange you see a possible threat.

Paranoid

If you are paranoid (or hyperaware), you are scared for no good reason. This is not the same as being aware. Being aware should make you more confident because you are seeing what is going on with your eyes, listening with your ears and being sensible with your mind. Being paranoid is when you let your imagination take over and you become scared when there is no obvious sign of danger rather than truly listening to your instincts (your "gut feeling").

Palm Strikes

Palm strikes are open-handed strikes thrown in a straight line or on a curve. It is good to start with a palm when striking a focus mitt (boxer's punching pad).

Personal Space

Your personal space is the immediate area that is around you. It is where you know you are safe so long as an attacker cannot reach you. You only allow people you feel you can trust and you want into your personal space. Your personal space will be larger if you are dealing with an adult or someone who is much bigger than you. This is because they have a longer reach. Your personal space grows depending on the size of the person who is interacting with you. Remember to respect your personal space and respect others' personal space as well.

Positioning

Positioning in self-protection is about putting yourself in the best and safest place. This is the place where you feel most in control. For example, when you use the fence, you use your position to keep your distance, but holding your ground, to be ready to act if you feel things are going to get physical (see also Offsetting). If you are in the middle of a fight and are grappling you might use positioning to get around your attacker's back, where you are in control.

Pre-emption

In self-protection this means to do something before your attacker does. This can mean avoiding eye contact with someone who looks like they are looking for trouble or it might mean striking an attacker before they strike you, such as when they try to invade your personal space.

Pressure Testing

You need to do activities with people who are genuinely testing you. This must be done in a safe way under adult supervision but what you use in self-defence needs to be tested. It is okay to try and fail during these tests. In fact, if you don't fail at least a few times, you are probably not being tested enough. Through testing we build the will to keep going under pressure and also what works for us.

Proactivity

In self-protection this means taking charge of you. When applied in self-defence it means to keep using your physical skills against your attacker until you can escape and to not wait for their reactions.

Punching

A punch is a strike used with a fist, hitting with the biggest set of knuckles. A punch can be thrown in a straight line or on a curve.

Red, Code

This is a state of awareness where you realise you are faced with a real physical threat. If you have been in code yellow and code orange you will be better prepared for the threat. If you were in code white then it will probably be too late.

Respect

Have respect for yourself and others. By having this attitude people have fewer reasons to pick on you. Bullies mostly either have a go at people they think are shy or people they feel "were asking for it" - in other words cocky people who are disrespectful to others. If you have respect for yourself, you will believe in yourself enough to stand up to the bully and not fall for his tricks. If you have respect for others, then it is less likely that you will upset people and give them a "reason" to pick on you.

Strategy

This is your overall action plan. You should have a simple plan that works and can be adapted to most situations. This book offers an overall self-protection plan.

Striking

Also known as hitting or beating. You can strike with many different parts of your body, but the most effective are your hands, elbows, head, knees, shins and feet. To get maximum force out of your strike you need to train to put all your bodyweight into all your strikes. However, whilst you are still growing, it is not advised to hit with full force on a regular basis. Instead train for accuracy, technique and speed.

Stamping

Stamps are best delivered with the heel of the foot to the top of your attacker's foot or ankle when they have hold of you. This should only be practised under the instruction of a good self-defence teacher.

Tactics

These are your short plans that come from your strategies. A tactic when faced by a threat might be using avoidance or to escape if you can. If you can't, your tactics might be to stun and run.

Takedowns and Throws

Takedowns and throws are grappling methods used to unbalance an attacker. The most common ones are simple trips, headlock takedowns and rugby or American football tackles. Throws are distinguished from takedowns by being much larger actions and possibly presenting greater risks to both fighters. However, remember that when you use a takedown or throw, you will most probably end up on the ground with your attacker. The ground is not a good place to be in a real life fight. Takedowns should only be practised under the supervision of a good self-defence or martial arts teacher.

Voice

Voice can be one of the most effective weapons you have. However, you must use it correctly. You might need to use it firmly if you feel someone is trying to control you through deception. You might need to use it to calm an angry person down. You might need to use it to throw aggression at someone when you use the angry fence. Finally, you might need to use it to call for help or to explain clearly to adults you trust what has happened.

Weapons

The best weapon you can have is your mind. If you carry a knife (or anything that it can be argued was intended to be used as a weapon) you are more likely to be injured in a real situation and get into trouble with the police. If someone uses a weapon, and you cannot immediately escape, use anything around you as a weapon. These incidental weapons should be chosen to give you distance and/or as shields as you make your escape. Again, it is important to train this under the guidance of a qualified teacher.

White, Code

Code white is the state of being unaware. You are switched off in this state and will not see an attack coming. However, we all go into code white no matter how hard we train. This isn't always a bad thing. For example, we cannot really be in code white when we go to sleep. We need time to completely rest. The important thing here is to do your best to ensure you are secure and safe before switching off.

Will

This is your inner strength to survive and succeed in whatever you do. In self-protection you need to have determination to survive.

Yellow, Code

Code yellow is the state of being aware. You are switched on and can see what is going on around you. You should be in code yellow most of the time.

Clubb Chimera Martial Arts

Realistic Self-Protection for
Children & Young People

Jamie Clubb is known for introducing realistic self-protection training to children. The CCMA (Clubb Chimera Martial Arts) method is a simple and easy-to-learn system of self-protection based on natural instinct and critical thinking. Children get honest feedback from the very beginning with safe and well-organised pressure-testing sessions that are both practical and fun.

CCMA workshops, webinars, presentations, seminars, webinars and private lessons can be booked through the Clubb Chimera Martial Arts website: **www.clubbchimera.com**

Thank You

I hope you have enjoyed reading this book.

Please tell your friends about it, or write a review online, or mention it on your favourite social networking site.

Acknowledgements

The creation of this totally updated version of "When Parents Aren't Around" owes a lot to the kind support of my friends, colleagues and family. Thanks to Thomas Wilson for agreeing to edit my book. Thomas, a lifelong friend since primary school and now a full-time professional educator, not only gave the book a thorough edit but also made some great new suggestions; one of these was that I write the "What Happens Afterwards" chapter. Tom was there right from the beginning with my own formal training in martial arts and self-protection and has remained a true friend in the most genuine sense of the word.

I would also like to thank another professional educator and the head of the Athena School of Karate, Mary Stevens. Mary not only gave my updated manuscript another sweep and polish but also helped organise the photography. She took photos, involved her students and set up the main shoot. Christopher Webb, head of Grove Martial Arts was also brought into the shoot with some of his students, including Chris Mort, one of his instructors and also father of one of the models featured. Students from both Athena and Grove did their teachers proud and were a true credit to the ethos of their respective schools, showing patience, understanding, interest, knowledge and an honest desire to make these shoots go well. Thanks to both clubs for your time, enthusiasm and input.

Robert Ager-Hutton published the first edition of "When Parents Aren't Around" as an eBook through his Ex-L-Ence Publishing in 2017. I am grateful to Robert for editing the first manuscript and for his belief in the project. Going back further, ex-school teacher and my father's old friend, Ian Lewis, kindly gave the original book its first edit and also gave me some good advice on the content.

The book was originally conceived at Disneyland, Paris in the winter of 2007 where I was one of a group of people involved in the creation of a European Martial Arts Festival. Outside of the meetings, the head of Summersdale Publishing's production arm, Nick Atkinson, suggested I write the first book on realistic children's self-protection. My thanks to Nick, for getting me to actually write what you have now hopefully read.

Along the way there have been some brilliant people who leant their credentials and support for a book that took a decade to publish. These include author, teacher and anti-bullying expert, Robert Higgs.

The book would not have been discussed in the first place if I hadn't made the decision at the formation of Clubb Chimera Martial Arts to teach realistic self-protection to young people. My gratitude here extends to all the martial arts teachers, school teachers, club captains, society representatives and pioneering parents who booked me to teach courses, seminars, private lessons and workshops in the UK and abroad, face-to-face and online. These services would not have been possible without the formative work in my regular classes in Kenilworth and Coventry. Here I would like to thank all my young students (now all grown up) and their parents for believing in my concepts when I first began teaching them in 2004.

Finally, I would like to thank my family for their kind support and belief throughout this journey. My love and gratitude to you all would fill its own book.

Photography Credits

Models:

<u>Athena School of Karate</u>
Amaya De Silva
Shenara De Silva
Mary Stevens
Mahdi Mecheri
Nasim Mecheri
Radka Mecheri
John Wamani
Joseph Wamani

<u>Grove Martial Arts</u>
Joseph Eason
Savannah Eason
Chris Mort
Emily Mort
Christopher Webb
Georgie Webb

Photographers:

Jamie Clubb
Chris Mort
Mary Stevens
Christopher Webb

Archive Photography
Miriam Clubb originally took the photographs that appear in the Code Orange and Code Red sections with Jamie Clubb and Gianni Susassi appearing as models in the "A Special Chapter on

Awareness" chapter (see below). They were originally taken in 2004 for several Kenilworth newspapers but have since ended up circling the internet and been reused by various children's self-defence schools. They feature my stepson, Gianni Susassi and me as the models. I decided to republish them in memory of my first children's self-protection classes and to set the record straight.

Printed in Great Britain
by Amazon

19202643R00068